D0516840

The Companion Guide to
Family Tree Maker®

TANA L. PEDERSEN

Copyright © 2007–2013
Ancestry.com Operations, Inc.
360 West 4800 North
Provo, Utah 84604
All rights reserved.

Ancestry.com and Family Tree Maker are registered trademarks of
Ancestry.com Operations, Inc.

All brand and product names are trademarks or
registered trademarks of their respective companies.
No part of this publication may be reproduced in any form
without written permission of the publisher, except by a reviewer, who may
quote brief passages for review.

Contents

Contents

Contents

Chapter 10   Running Reports 149

Contents

Chapter 11　Creating a Family History Book 175

Part Four: Managing Your Trees 193

Chapter 12　Working with Trees 195

Chapter 13   Tools and Preferences 217

Introduction

Congratulations on selecting Family Tree Maker to discover and preserve your family's heritage. It's easy to use for those just starting to research their family history, but it's also robust enough for the most serious genealogist. Use Family Tree Maker to store, display, and share any kind of family information—from names, marriages, and deaths to priceless family stories, photos, and videos.

This guide is designed to help you learn Family Tree Maker quickly, leaving you more time to discover your family history. Even if you have never used a genealogy program before, you'll find that the features in Family Tree Maker make it possible to keep track of even the most tangled of family trees.

This book is written with the novice computer user in mind. You'll read about many of the useful tools that the casual Family Tree Maker user never discovers, and you'll be taken on a hands-on trip through the program. The many illustrations let you check your progress as you master each new feature or concept. Even if you are familiar with computers, though, you may have only recently been introduced to Family Tree Maker or simply want to know what great features you have not yet discovered in the program. This book offers you a step-by-step tour of the program and all that you can accomplish with it.

Before you begin entering your family's information, be sure to check out the "Family Tree Maker Basics" chapter. It will give you the skills you need to navigate through Family Tree Maker and will familiarize you with the software's interface.

What's New?

Organizing and sharing your family history is easier with new features and report enhancements.

- **User requests.** Based on your feedback, we're including several widely requested features in this version of Family Tree Maker: a new family view of your tree has been added to the People workspace (similar to the family view in Ancestry.com trees); media items can be marked as private so they won't be exported or displayed in your online tree; a new global sort tool lets you display all children in your tree by birth order (you can still manually choose a sort order for specific families); and a new option simplifies exporting a single branch of your family tree.

- **TreeSync™ improvements.** Numerous changes make TreeSync faster and even more reliable. It's also easier to keep your online and desktop trees synced if you encounter an issue; previously, if you had to use a backup file, your tree wouldn't sync anymore and you'd have to upload a new version. Now you can back up a synced tree and restore it if you have any problems. You can also print a list of your sync changes.

- **New organizational tool for places.** The larger your tree gets, the more locations you have to keep track of. Now, on the Places workspace, locations can be grouped together by country, state, county, and city to make them easier to look at and sort through.

- **New and improved reports.** Family Tree Maker has several new reports. The new Family View Report lets you display an individual's ancestors, spouses, and children together (similar to the family group view on the People workspace). The new Undocumented Facts Report lists facts that have no sources associated with them. The Index of Individuals Report has been expanded to include anniversary, birthday, and contact lists. In addition, there have been dozens of performance improvements and enhancements to all reports.

- **New media viewer.** The media viewer has been updated to display PDFs and has a new magnifying tool so you can get close-up views of your images.

- **More options when editing facts.** No more manually creating facts for multiple family members—now you can copy and paste facts to as many relatives as you like. Best of all, the copied fact will include any associated source citations, media items, and notes. Also, if you have multiple versions of the same fact, you can merge them together without losing any information.

- **Improved backups.** In the past, if you spent time setting up website favorites or creating historical events for timelines, you lost this information if you had to delete your tree and use a backup. Now this information can be included in a backup file. Media files can also be backed up regardless of where they're located on your hard drive.

How the Guide Is Organized

As you read this book, you'll notice several features that provide you with useful information:

- Tips give you advice on the best ways to perform tasks.

- Notes offer you timely hints and explanations about how features work.

- Sidebars give you additional information on a variety of family history topics, such as using maps, that will enhance your ability to create a richer and more complete family tree.

- A glossary explains words you might not be familiar with, such as Family Tree Maker terms (family group view, Fastfields), and genealogy terms (GEDCOM, Ahnentafel).

If you still need help, a quick perusal of the Table of Contents should lead you right to the task you are trying to perform; if not, check the index in the back of the book.

Part One
Getting Started

Chapter One
Installing Family Tree Maker

This chapter lists the system requirements for Family Tree Maker, shows you how to install the software, and gives a quick introduction to the available help resources.

Recommended System Requirements

To use Family Tree Maker, you'll need a computer that meets the following specifications. Keep in mind that the more information in your tree, the greater the amount of free hard drive space and available RAM you will necd. If you have lots of images or videos, you'll need a substantial amount of hard drive space.

- Operating system: Microsoft Windows® XP SP2/Vista® (32-bit or 64-bit)/Windows® 7 (32-bit or 64-bit)/Windows® 8 (32-bit or 64-bit)
- Processor: 1GHz Intel Pentium® III (or equivalent)
- Hard disk space: 675MB for installation
- Memory: 1GB RAM
- Display: 1024x768 resolution monitor
- DVD drive

All online features require Internet access. User is responsible for Internet Service Provider (ISP) account, all Internet access fees, and phone charges.

Installing Family Tree Maker

To use Family Tree Maker, the software must be installed on your computer's hard drive; you cannot run it directly from the DVD. If you have an earlier version installed on your computer, this new version will not copy over it. While the installation process will not harm your existing Family Tree Maker trees, it's always a good idea to back up your files on a flash drive, CD, or DVD before beginning.

1. Insert the Family Tree Maker installation disc into your computer's DVD drive.

   - If the AutoPlay window opens, click **Run setup.exe**. (If the User Account Control window opens, click **Yes** to continue.)

   - If the installer doesn't start automatically, click the Windows **Start** button and select **Computer**. Double-click the icon for your DVD drive. (If the User Account Control window opens, click **Yes** to continue.)

2. Follow the on-screen instructions to complete the installation.

   Note: If you experience any difficulties, please see the troubleshooting chapter.

Registering the Software

Before you create your first tree, take a minute to register the software. Registered users get the following benefits: the powerful Web Search feature, the ability to add Ancestry.com records to your trees; discounts on future versions of Family Tree Maker; and notifications of software updates.

Make sure your computer is connected to the Internet. From the **Help** menu, select **Register Family Tree Maker**. Then follow the on-screen instructions.

Activating an Ancestry.com Subscription

If you're already a member of Ancestry.com, or if a trial membership came with your Family Tree Maker purchase, you can activate your subscription in the software.

Make sure your computer is connected to the Internet. From the **Help** menu, select **Activate Ancestry Subscription**. Then follow the on-screen instructions.

License Agreement

Please read the license agreement. You can view it during the software installation or at a later time. The *License* text file is located in the same folder on your hard drive where you installed Family Tree Maker.

Getting Help

Family Tree Maker has a built-in Help system, tutorials, and online technical support. If you have questions about a feature or simply want to learn more about the program, check out one of these resources.

Help Program

To access Help, go to the **Help** menu and select **Help for Family Tree Maker**; or press the **F1** key and click the **Show** button. Use these tabs on the Help window (fig. 1-1) to find the topic you're interested in:

- **Contents tab.** Click to view topics arranged in chapters, like a book's table of contents.

- **Index tab.** Click to view topics by words and phrases.

- **Search tab.** Click to look for specific words or phrases within Help topics. Many useful topic pages can be found by entering keywords such as "adding," "creating," and "merging."

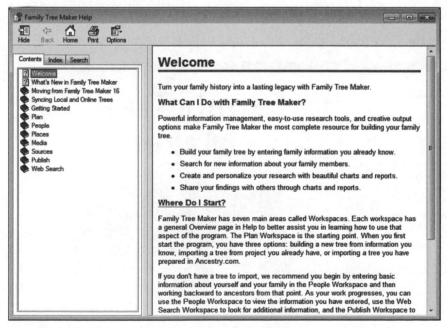

Figure 1-1. The Welcome window in the Help program.

Navigating in the Help Program

The Help program uses blue, underlined links to take you to related topics. Simply click on any link to go to a new topic. Use these options to move around within the Help program:

- **Hide/Show.** Click to show and hide the tab view of the Help window.

- **Back/Forward.** Click to return to Help pages you've viewed already.

- **Print.** Click to print the currently selected Help page.

- **Options button.** Click to display a sub-menu of additional options, such as "Search Highlight On," which you can use to highlight search terms on a Help page.

Tutorials

Family Tree Maker includes a variety of tutorials that illustrate and explain how to use the software. You will quickly learn how to organize, research, and share your family history.

1. From the **Help** menu, select **Training Tutorials**.

2. When the video player opens, click a topic to launch its tutorial.

Ancestry.com Blog

The Ancestry.com blog has the latest company news, information about search-ing for your ancestors, tips on using Family Tree Maker, and more. Want to know when the next webinar is? Interested in seeing which collections were just added? Go to blogs.ancestry.com. And don't forget to leave your own comments and questions.

Companion Guide

To view this *Companion Guide* as a PDF, select **Companion Guide** from the **Help** menu. (If you are unable to open the PDF, you may need to install Adobe Reader, which is available as a free download from the Adobe website at www.adobe.com.)

Technical Support

Family Tree Maker has an Online Help Center, where you can get help for technical problems and answers to customer service questions. You'll also find easy-to-understand articles, tips, and step-by-step instructions. Select **Online Help Center** from the **Help** menu or go to www.familytreemaker.com.

If you still have questions, you can call 1-800-ANCESTRY (1-800-262-3787) to talk to our experienced support staff—available seven days a week from 10 a.m. to 10 p.m. (EST). You can also email questions to support@ancestry.com.

Customer Experience Program

If you'd like to help improve Family Tree Maker, you can participate in the customer experience program. The software will automatically send information about how you use the program and how it's performing. To join select **Customer Experience** from the **Help** menu. Click **Yes, I want to participate**; then click **OK**.

Chapter Two
Family Tree Maker Basics

Family Tree Maker makes it easy—and enjoyable—for anyone to discover their family history and gather it into one convenient location. And whether you're interested in printing family charts to share at a reunion or looking for an easy way to store your family facts, photos, and records, Family Tree Maker is the program to help you do it all.

This chapter gives you the basic skills and knowledge you need to launch the program and navigate around the software. Let's get started.

Opening and Closing Family Tree Maker

To open the program double-click the **Family Tree Maker 2014** icon on your computer desktop or click the Windows **Start** button and select **Family Tree Maker 2014**.

To close the program click **File>Exit** or click the **Close** button (**X**) in the upper-right corner. Remember, there's no need to save your tree—Family Tree Maker automatically saves changes as you make them.

The Family Tree Maker Interface

To use any computer program effectively, the first step is to understand its unique interface and tools. You'll immediately recognize many common features in Family Tree Maker. However, there are some toolbars, menus, and windows you'll want to learn how to use.

Toolbars

The main toolbar in Family Tree Maker (fig. 2-1) is located at the top of the window above the menu bar. It provides quick navigation to various workspaces—groupings of the most important features in the software. On the far left you'll find the Select Tree button that lets you switch between trees.

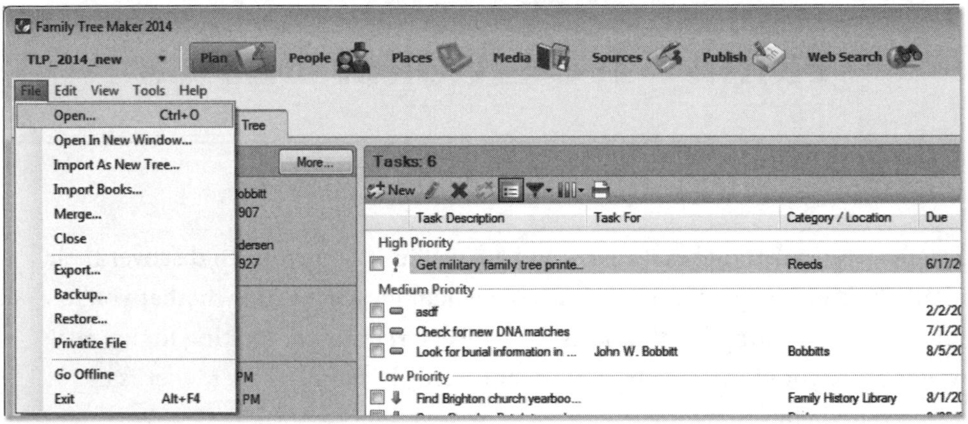

Figure 2-1. The main toolbar and menu bar.

Menus and Keyboard Shortcuts

Family Tree Maker menus work like any other computer program. Simply click a menu name to display its options; then, click the option you want. Some menu options have keyboard shortcuts that allow you to access features without using the mouse.

Workspaces Overview

Family Tree Maker groups important features together in workspaces. Each workspace has a slightly different appearance and purpose, but generally, they all contain the same elements, such as toolbars and tabs.

The Plan Workspace

The Plan workspace is the "control center" where you manage your family trees. On the New Tree tab you can start a new tree, import an existing file, or download a tree from Ancestry.com.

The Current Tree tab on the Plan workspace (fig. 2-2) lets you view details about your tree, manage your research to-do list, and, if you've linked your

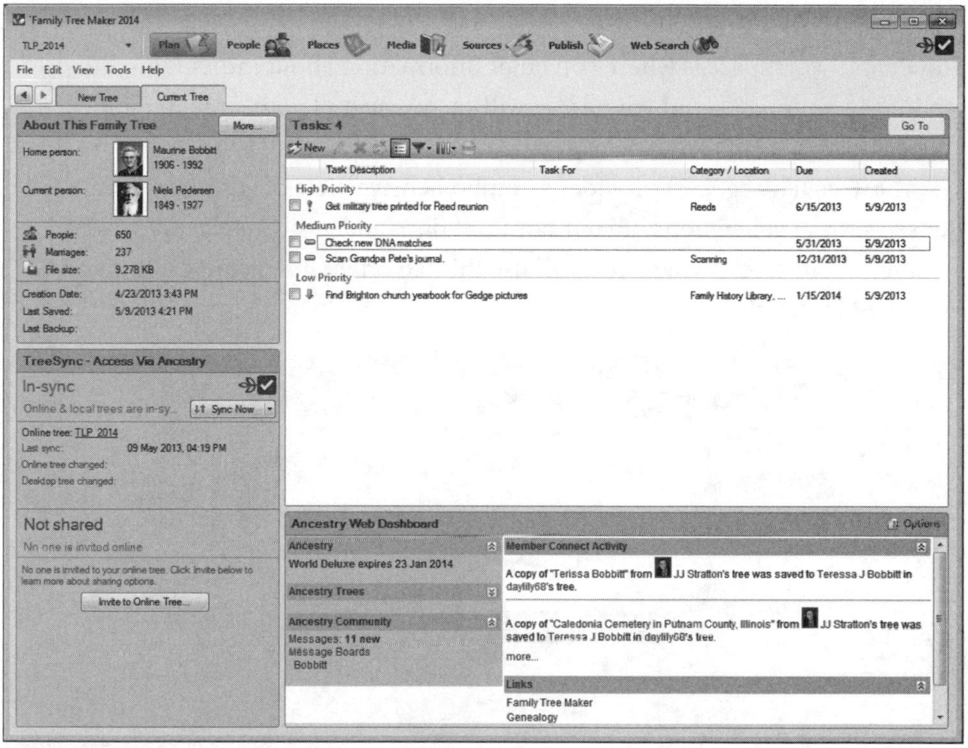

Figure 2-2. The Current Tree tab on the Plan workspace.

desktop tree to an online tree, you can also manage how often the trees are synced. This tab also contains the Web Dashboard, where you can access your Ancestry account and Member Trees, get email notifications, and view Member Connect activity.

What Is Member Connect?

Member Connect helps you stay in touch with others who are researching your ancestors. Ancestry.com scans public Member Trees and notifies you when there's activity around records you've saved or commented on.

The People Workspace

The People workspace is where you enter information about individuals and families in your tree—and where you will spend most of your time in Family Tree Maker.

The Tree tab (fig. 2-3) provides a comprehensive view of your family. You can see several generations of your family at once and easily navigate to each person in your tree. Because you will use this tab often, its various sections are explained in detail.

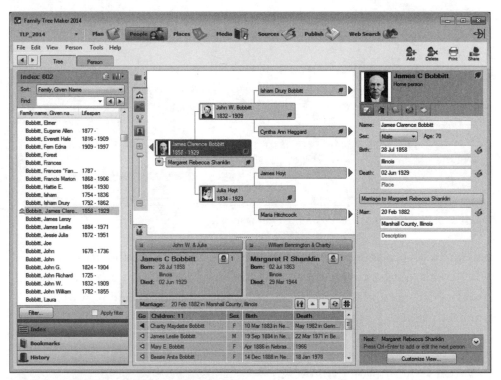

Figure 2-3. The Tree tab on the People workspace.

The Index

The Index (fig. 2-4) lists all the individuals in your tree and is one of the easiest ways to locate the person you want to focus on. To view information for a specific individual, simply click his or her name in the Index. If you can't see the person you want, use the scroll bar to move up and down the list, or type a name in the Find field to jump to a particular person.

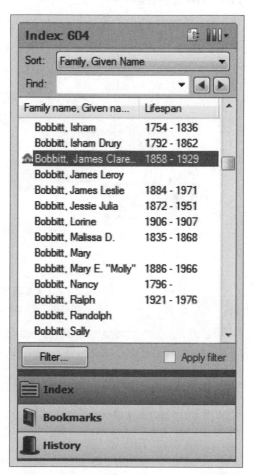

The house icon indicates the individual who is the current home person in the tree. (You'll learn more about the home person in chapter 3.)

To make it easier to locate individuals, you can change how the Index sorts names using the **Sort** drop-down list. Also, you can add birth, marriage, or death dates by clicking the **Show additional data** button.

You can also limit the Index so it displays only certain individuals; click the **Filter** button and choose a specific family line, an individual's descendants, or a group of your choice. Click the

Figure 2-4. The Index.

Bookmarks button to see a list of individuals you have specifically bookmarked, or click the **History** button to see the individuals you have added or edited recently.

The Tree Viewer

The tree viewer (fig. 2-5) helps you navigate your family tree as well as enter new individuals.

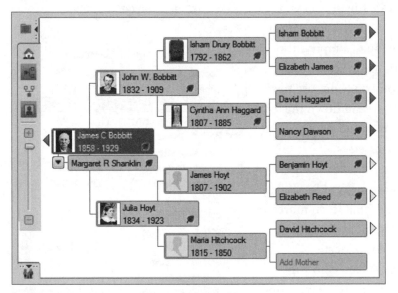

Figure 2-5. The pedigree view in the tree viewer.

These buttons will help you use the tree viewer:

 Go to home person. Makes the home person the primary individual or focus of the tree.

 Pedigree view. Shows a pedigree view of your tree. The primary individual or focus of the tree is on the left, with ancestors branching out to the right.

 Family view. Shows a family view of your tree. The primary individual is at the base of the tree, with ancestors branching above the individual— paternal on the left and maternal on the right.

 Include pictures. Displays portraits and life spans for each individual on the pedigree view.

 Re-center on selected person. Adjusts the tree to focus on the currently selected person on the family view.

The Family Group View

The family group view (fig. 2-6) lets you view an individual's spouse and children. Click the "parents" button above the individual to display his or her parents and siblings. The toolbar buttons let you edit the couple's marriage fact, change the display order of their children, and view blended families.

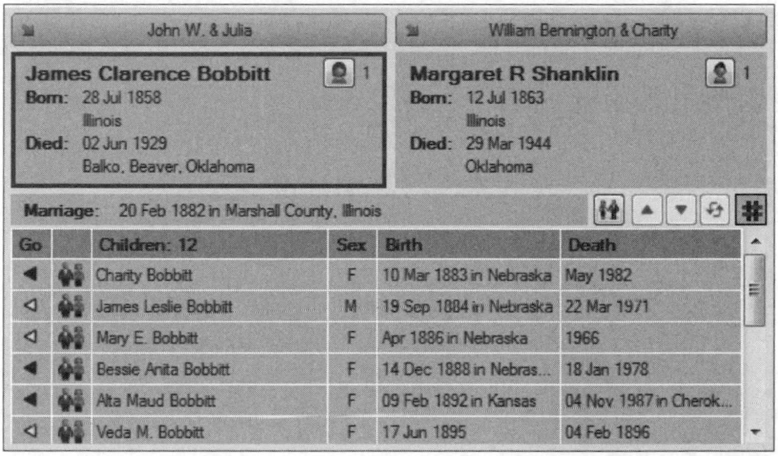

Figure 2-6. The family group view on the People workspace.

The Editing Panel

The editing panel (fig. 2-7) is where you'll enter basic information about an individual, such as birth, marriage, and death dates and places. At the top you'll find a portrait of an individual (if you've added one) and how he or she is related to the home person. Toolbar buttons under the portrait let you display media items, notes, Web links, and tasks associated with the individual.

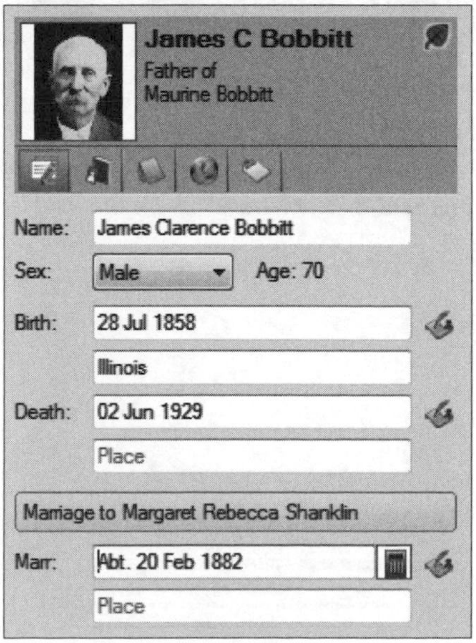

Figure 2-7. The editing panel.

The Person Tab

The Person tab on the People workspace (fig. 2-8) lets you add facts, media items, Web links, and notes for an individual. You can also view a timeline for an individual and their relationships to other family members.

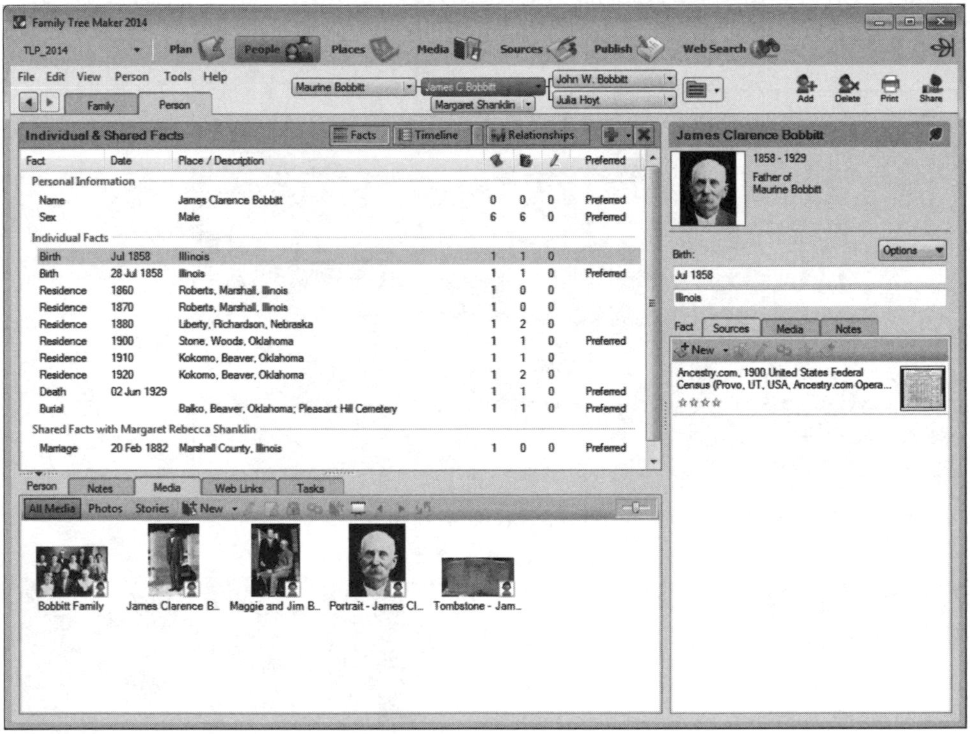

Figure 2-8. The Person tab on the People workspace.

The Places Workspace

The Places workspace (fig. 2-9) helps you view the locations you've entered for events—and gives you the opportunity to view online maps of them. The Places panel on the left shows every location you've entered in your tree. When you click on a place, it will be displayed in the map at the center of the workspace. The details panel on the right side shows the individuals who have life events associated with the location. You can also view locations as a migration path by choosing a person from the List by drop-down.

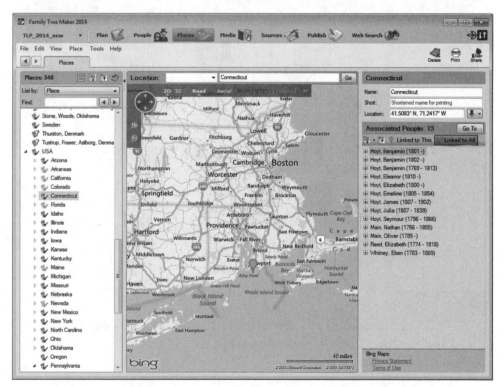

Figure 2-9. The Places workspace.

The Media Workspace

The Media workspace acts as a storage space for your photos, audio recordings, movies, family documents, and historical records. On the Media Collection tab (fig. 2-10) you can view thumbnails of your media items and enter information about them. On the Media Detail tab you can add notes for an item and link it to individuals and sources.

Figure 2-10. The Collection tab on the Media workspace.

The Sources Workspace

The Sources workspace (fig. 2-11) organizes your sources and source citations. The Source Groups panel on the left lets you sort sources by person, title, and repository; the sources display area shows which citations have been entered for a specific source. Tabs at the bottom of the window show the individuals linked to a source citation, related notes, and media items. In the editing panel you can enter or update specific source citations.

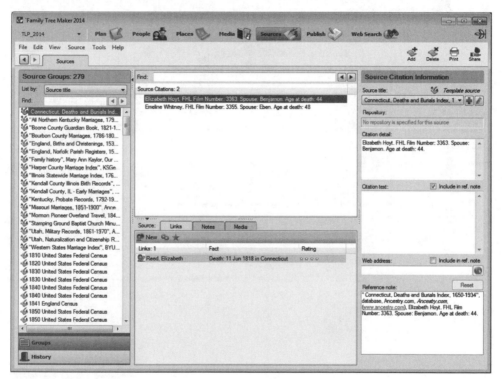

Figure 2-11. The Sources workspace.

The Publish Workspace

The Publish workspace offers a variety of charts and reports that you can view, print, and share. You can also create family history books. The Publish Collection tab (fig. 2-12) shows the types of charts and reports that are available and gives an explanation of each.

On the Publish Detail tab you can customize a chart or report using the editing panel.

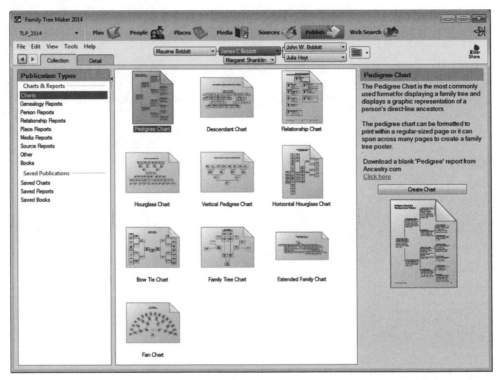

Figure 2-12. The Collection tab on the Publish workspace.

The Web Search Workspace

The Web Search workspace (fig. 2-13) lets you search billions of records on Ancestry.com to find more information about your relatives—all without leaving Family Tree Maker. You can also search other websites and easily download discoveries into your tree with the Web-clipping tool.

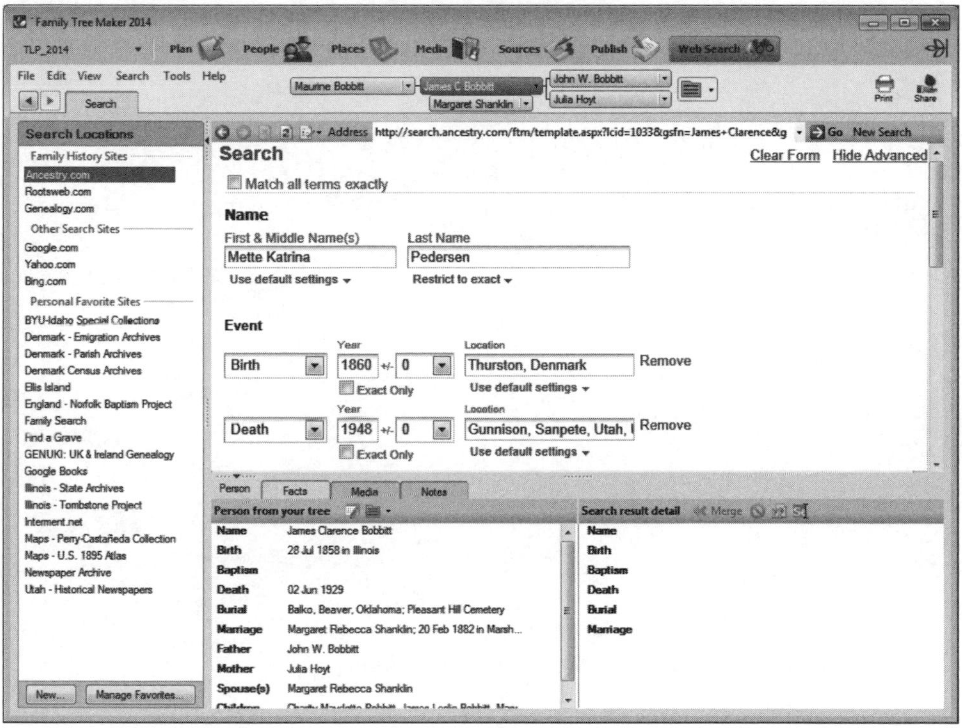

Figure 2-13. The Web Search workspace.

Chapter Three
Creating a Tree

Before You Begin

This chapter assumes that you have installed Family Tree Maker and read chapters 1 and 2. Once you've learned a few of the basic Family Tree Maker features, you're ready to create your first tree. Make sure you have family information handy or have a file, such as a GEDCOM or Ancestry.com tree, to use.

How Many Trees Should You Create?

When most beginners create a family tree, their first question is, "Should I create one large, all-inclusive tree or several small trees, one for each family?" The truth is, there is no right answer.

The advantages to having one large tree are pretty clear. One computer file is easier to keep track of—one file to enter your information in, one file to back up, one file to share. Also, you won't have to duplicate your efforts by entering some data, sources, and media items in several trees.

Multiple trees can be useful too. The more trees you have, the smaller the files will typically be. If you have concerns about your computer's performance or have storage issues, smaller files might work best. Smaller files also make it easier to collaborate with other family members; you can send them only the family lines they're interested in.

Regardless of which way you organize your trees initially, don't feel like you're stuck with a permanent decision. The flexible nature of Family Tree Maker means you can merge files any time; you can even export parts of your tree to create a brand new tree.

Creating a Tree

A tree is where you gather and enter your family facts and details. If you've received a family history file from another family member or researcher, you can import the file, creating a new tree. Then, you can begin adding your own information. You can also create a tree by entering a few quick facts about yourself or by downloading a tree you've created on Ancestry.com.

Entering Your Information from Scratch

If this is your first time creating a family tree, you'll want to use this option. Enter a few facts about yourself and your parents, and you're on your way.

1. Click the **Plan** button on the main toolbar to open the Plan workspace.

2. On the New Tree tab, click **Enter What You Know**.

3. Type your name and choose your gender. You can also enter your birth date and place and your parents' names.

```
Start a New Tree

Let's start by entering what you know.
                            Father's name:
 ⓘ Name:                    Thomas Wentworth
 Marie Wentworth            Mother's name:
 Sex:                       Cynthia James
   [        ▼]
                                              New tree name:
 Birth date:     Birthplace:                  Wentworth Family
 17 Mar 1958     Harrington, Kent, Delaware      [ Continue ]

 [ File Location... ]   C:\Users\tlord\Documents\Family Tree Maker\Wentworth Family.ftm
```

4. Enter a name for the tree in the **New tree name** field.

5. By default, your tree will be saved to a Family Tree Maker folder located in your documents folder. If you want to save the file to another folder, click **File Location**.

   Note: You cannot save a tree to a floppy disk or CD; your tree must be on your hard drive while you're working on it. But, you can save a backup of your tree to a removable drive or CD.

6. Click **Continue**. The tree opens to the People workspace, where you can start entering your family information.

Importing a Tree

If you've already created a tree or received one from another family member, you can import it. Previous versions of Family Tree Maker, GEDCOMs (GEnealogical Data COMmunications format), FamilySearch™ Personal Ancestral Files (PAFs), *Legacy Family Tree* files, and *The Master Genealogist* files are all compatible.

1. If you haven't already, copy the tree you want to import to your computer's hard drive.

2. Click the **Plan** button on the main toolbar to open the Plan workspace.

3. On the New Tree tab, click **Import an Existing Tree**.

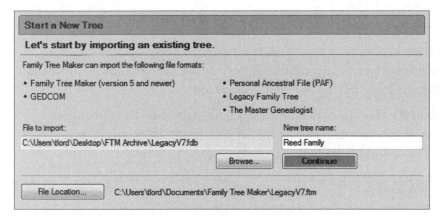

4. Click **Browse** to locate the file you want to import.

5. By default, your tree will be saved to a Family Tree Maker folder located in your documents folder. If you want to save the file to another folder, click **File Location**.

6. If necessary, change the file's name in the **New tree name** field.

7. Click **Continue**. You'll see the Import Complete window, which shows statistics for the new tree, including the number of individuals, families, and sources that were imported.

8. Click **Close**. The tree opens to the People workspace, where you can start entering your family information.

Downloading a Tree from Ancestry.com

If you've created a tree on Ancestry.com, you don't need to start over in Family Tree Maker; you can download the tree to your desktop. It will include all the facts, sources, and images you've manually attached to individuals.

Note: To download an Ancestry tree, you must be the tree's owner; you can't download trees you've been invited to view or share.

Downloading and Linking a Tree in Family Tree Maker

When you download a tree from Ancestry.com, you can create a link between your online Ancestry tree and its corresponding tree on your desktop. This means that additions, deletions, or edits you make in your Family Tree Maker tree will be duplicated in your Ancestry tree (and vice versa). (For more information see "Working with Linked Trees" on page 208.)

Note: When you download and link a tree in Family Tree Maker, you must create a new tree; you cannot merge it with another tree.

1. Make sure you are logged in to your Ancestry.com account (if necessary click the login link on the Plan workspace).

2. Go to the New Tree tab on the Plan workspace and click **Download a Tree from Ancestry**. Make sure the Link to Ancestry checkbox is selected. A list of your trees appears.

Start a New Tree				

Let's start by downloading your online tree from Ancestry.

☑ Link to Ancestry

Download and link your Ancestry Member Tree to a new tree in Family Tree Maker. When trees are linked, changes made to either tree are copied to the other. A tree can be downloaded without being linked, in which case the two trees have no connection to each other.

Refresh

Ancestry Tree Name ▲	Created	Last Modified	Status	Action	
Mains of New England	20 Sep 2012	21 Sep 2012	Not linked to this machine	Download...	
Pedersen-Reed	31 Jul 2006	07 Mar 2013	Not linked to this machine	Download...	✖

3. Click **Download** next to the appropriate tree.

4. If you want to change the name of the tree, enter the new name in the **Family Tree Maker filename** field.

5. Choose whether your online and desktop trees will be synced manually or automatically. (For help see "Setting Up Syncing" on page 208.)

   Note: The first time you download an Ancestry tree, you'll choose the type of Internet connection you're using. This helps Family Tree Maker download your tree more efficiently.

6. Click the **Download citation media** checkbox to also download all Ancestry record images attached to your tree.

   Note: You may not want to download images if you have a slow Internet connection or have limited space on your hard drive.

7. Click **Continue**. When the tree has been downloaded successfully, click **Close**.

Downloading a Tree to Family Tree Maker Without Linking

You can download a tree from Ancestry.com without creating a link between it and your desktop Family Tree Maker tree. Use it to create a new desktop tree or merge it with a different tree.

1. Make sure you are logged in to your Ancestry.com account (if necessary click the login link on the Plan workspace).

2. Go to the New Tree tab on the Plan workspace and click **Download a Tree from Ancestry**. Make sure the Link to Ancestry checkbox is *not* selected. A list of your trees appears.

3. Click **Export** next to the appropriate tree.

Start a New Tree		
Let's start by downloading your online tree from Ancestry.		
☐ Link to Ancestry		
Mains of New England	9/21/2012	Export
Pedersen-Reed	3/7/2013	Export

Note: The first time you download an Ancestry tree, you'll choose the type of Internet connection you're using. This helps Family Tree Maker download your tree more efficiently.

4. Click **Download to Family Tree Maker**. A message asks whether you want to merge the Ancestry tree with an existing tree or create a new one.

5. Choose one of these options:

    • To save the file as a new tree, click **Import**. Then enter a name for the tree and save it.

    • To merge the file with an existing tree, click **Merge**. The Merge Wizard will guide you through combining the trees.

Choosing a Home Person

Each tree has a home person. By default, this is the first person you enter in a tree. If you're creating a tree based on your family, the home person will most likely be you. However, the home person can be anyone in your tree.

Occasionally, you may want to switch the home person. For example, if you're working on a specific family line, you may want to make someone in that ancestral line the home person.

Changing the Home Person on the Plan Workspace

1. Click the **Plan** button on the main toolbar and then click the **Current Tree** tab. At the top of the window, you'll see the name of the current home person.

2. Hover over "Home person" and click the button that appears.

3. In the Index of Individuals window, click the new home person and click **OK**.

Changing the Home Person on the People Workspace

1. Click the **People** button on the main toolbar; then click the **Tree** tab.

2. Find the appropriate person in the tree viewer or Index; then right-click the individual and click **Set As Home Person**.

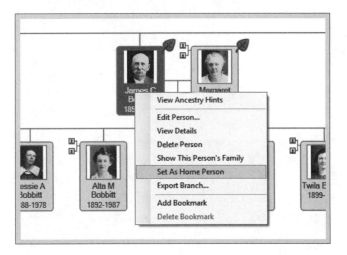

Part Two
Building a Tree

Chapter Four
Entering Family Information

Much of your time using Family Tree Maker will be spent entering the names, dates, and events that you've uncovered about your family. The simplest way to build your tree is to begin with what you already know—basic details about yourself, your spouse, your children, and your parents. As your tree grows, your focus can turn to ancestral lines, such as your grandparents and great-grandparents.

When you've entered basic birth, marriage, and death information for your family, you can expand your tree by adding marriage details, immigration stories, medical histories, and more.

Entering Basic Information for an Individual

You can enter facts about an individual (such as birth and death dates) on the Tree tab in the People workspace.

1. Click the **People** button on the main toolbar to open the People workspace.

2. Click an individual's name in the Index or tree viewer. The person's name and gender will be displayed in the editing panel.

3. In the editing panel, enter a date in the **Birth Date** field.

Entering Names

To keep names in your tree consistent, you'll want to follow these guidelines.

- Be sure to use a woman's maiden name (her last name before she was married). This helps you trace her family and keeps you from confusing her with other people in your tree.

- You may have last names (surnames) that are not a single word. You will need to identify these names with backslashes (\); otherwise, Family Tree Maker will read only the last word as the surname. Here are some examples:

George \de la Vergne\   Teresa \Garcia Ramirez\

4. Next, click the **Birth Place** field and type the location where the individual was born.

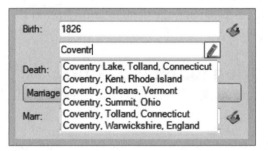

Tip: As you enter a location, you'll notice that a list of possible matches appears. To use a suggested location, click it; to ignore the suggestions, continue typing.

5. If you know an individual's death date and place, enter this too. You can now continue by adding marriage facts, entering additional family members, entering more facts for the individual, or adding photographs.

Entering Dates

Family Tree Maker automatically converts dates to the standard format used by genealogists: date, month, year. For example, 26 May 1961. If the program can't interpret the date you entered, a message asks for clarification. Simply retype the date in the standard format.

If you don't know the date for an event, you can leave the Date field blank or type "Unknown". If you have an approximate date, you can indicate this by typing "About 1920" or "Abt. 1920".

Adding a Spouse

1. Click **Add Spouse** in the family group view. In the field that appears, enter the spouse's name (first, middle, and last) and click **OK**. Don't forget to use maiden names for women.

2. Choose a gender from the drop-down list and click **OK**. The spouse is now the focus of the tree viewer and editing panel.

3. Enter any basic facts (such as birth and death) you have for the new spouse.

Entering Locations

Recording locations accurately and completely is an important part of your family history. Generally, you'll enter a location from the smallest to largest division. For example, in the United States, you would enter city or town, county, state, country (Haddam, Washington, Kansas, United States). For foreign locations, you would enter city or town, parish or district, province or county, country (Witton, Aston, Warwickshire, England).

To help you enter locations quickly and consistently, Family Tree Maker has a locations database that includes more than 3 million place names. When you type a location, Family Tree Maker checks the name against the database and suggests possible matches. You can select a location from the list or add your own place names.

Entering Details About a Relationship

After you've entered a spouse for an individual, you'll want to include any additional information you have about the couple. You can entered shared facts (such as marriage or divorce), notes, and media items (such as wedding photos).

1. Go to the **Tree** tab on the People workspace and select the appropriate individual.

2. To add a marriage date and place, simply enter the information in the appropriate fields.

> Marriage to Sarah Thompson
>
> Marr: 27 Jan 1845
>
> Aston, Warwickshire, England
>
> Parish Church of St Peter and St Paul

3. To enter more information for the couple, click the **Marriage to** button; then click a tab to enter facts, notes, or media items.

Adding a Child to a Family

1. In the family group view, click **Add Child**. Then, enter the child's name (first, middle, and last) and click **OK**.

Tip: Family Tree Maker assumes that a child has the same last name as the father and automatically fills it in for you. You can ignore the suggested name by typing over it.

2. In the editing panel, choose a gender and enter any birth and death information you have for the child.

Changing the Sort Order of Children

You can change the order in which children appear in the family group view, for example your direct ancestor can be displayed at the top of the list regardless of his or her birth order, or you can display all children by birth order.

1. Go to the **Tree** tab on the People workspace and select the appropriate family.

2. Click a child in the family group view.

3. Do one of these options:

   - Click the **Move child up** and **Move child down** buttons to move a child to a specific place in the order.

   - Click the **Sort** button to display the children in their birth order. Choose whether you want to sort this family only or all children in your tree. Then click **OK**.

Adding Parents

When you've added your spouse and children to your tree, you'll want to continue with your parents, grandparents, great-grandparents, and so on.

1. Go to the **Tree** tab on the People workspace. In the Index or tree viewer, click the individual you want to add a father or mother to.

2. Click **Add Father** or **Add Mother** in the tree viewer.

3. Enter the parent's name (first, middle, and last). Don't forget to use maiden names for women.

4. In the editing panel, choose a gender and enter any birth and death information you have for the individual.

Adding More Details

So far you've only entered basic facts for a person. Now you can add more details and notes.

Adding a Fact

In addition to birth and death events, you can add facts such as christenings, immigration, and occupations.

Note: You'll want to record the source of each fact. A source is where you learned the information such as a book or historical record. For more information see chapter 5.

1. Go to the **Person** tab on the People workspace and select the appropriate individual.

2. Click the **Facts** button. The facts you've already entered for the person appear in the Individual and Shared Facts section.

3. Right-click the workspace and select **Add Fact,** or click the **Add fact** (+) button in the toolbar. The Add Fact window opens.

Add Fact		
Facts	**Type**	OK
Namesake	Individual	Cancel
Nationality	Individual	Help
Naturalization	Individual	
Nickname	Individual	
Obituary	Individual	New...
Occupation	Individual	
Ordinance	Individual	
Ordination	Individual	
Origin	Individual	
other	Individual	
Person ID	Individual	
Phone Number	Individual	
Physical Description	Individual	
Political Office	Individual	

4. Choose a fact from the list and click **OK**.

Tip: You can add your own fact types (for example, college graduation) by clicking the **New** button in the Add Fact window.

Notice that the editing panel on the right-hand side of the window displays the appropriate fields for the fact.

Occupation:	✔	Options ▼
1848		
Birmingham, Warwickshire, England		
Black leadmaker		

5. Complete the **Date**, **Place**, and **Description** fields as necessary.

Note: Don't forget to add a source for the fact. For instructions see "Creating Sources" on page 62.

Common Facts

In addition to birth, marriage, and death events, here are some facts you will probably encounter as you record your family history:

- **Address.** Addresses can be useful for keeping contact information for living relatives or for recording where an ancestor lived.

- **Also Known As.** Use this fact if an individual was known by a nickname rather than his or her given name.

- **Baptism and Christening.** Birth records are not always available, so christening records become useful because they may be the earliest available information you can find for an ancestor.

- **Burial.** If you can't find a death record for an individual, but you have a burial record, you can use this information to estimate a person's death date.

- **Cause of Death/Medical Condition.** Knowing your family's health history may help you prevent and treat illnesses that run in families. You can record an individual's cause of death or enter details you know about an individual's medical history, from long-term illness to simple things such as "suffers from allergies."

- **Emigration/Immigration.** Emigration and immigration records are the first step in finding your ancestors in their homeland. Use these facts to record dates, ports of departure and arrival, and even ship names.

- **Physical Description.** Although not necessarily beneficial to your research, a physical description of an ancestor can be a fascinating addition to any family history.

- **Title.** If an individual has a title, such as Captain, you can use it to tell the difference between this individual and others with the same or similar names.

Copying and Pasting Facts

You can copy a fact from one person and paste it into the facts for another person. This is useful if several family members share the same fact (such as residence), and you don't want to create a new fact for each person.

1. Go to the **Person** tab on the People workspace and select the appropriate individual.

2. Click the **Facts** button.

3. Right-click the fact you want to copy and select **Copy**.

4. Use the mini pedigree tree above the workspace to go the person you want to add the fact to.

5. Right-click the Individual & Shared Facts workspace and select **Paste**. A list of immediate family members appears.

6. Click the checkboxes next to each person you want to add the fact to; then click **OK**.

Adding Alternate Facts

As you add facts, you may discover conflicting information about the same life event, such as two birth dates. When you have multiple facts for the same event, one fact will be "preferred," and the others will be "alternates." In figure 4-1 the birth has one preferred fact and two alternate facts.

Individual & Shared Facts		Facts	Timeline	Relationships				
Fact	Date	Place / Description			🐾	📷	✏	Preferred
Personal Information								
Name		Joseph Gold			2	2	0	Preferred
Sex		Male			1	1	0	Preferred
Individual Facts								
Birth	Abt. 1824				0	0	0	
Birth	1825	Coventry, Warwickshire, England			1	1	0	Preferred
Birth	Abt. 1825	England			1	1	0	
Baptism	12 Sep 1825	Coventry, Warwickshire, England; St. John the Baptist			2	3	0	Preferred
Residence	1851	Birmingham, Warwickshire, England			1	1	0	Preferred
Shared Facts with Sarah Thompson								
Marriage	27 Jan 1845	Aston, Warwickshire, England; Parish Church of St Peter and ...		1	2	0		Preferred
Shared Facts with Martha Rogers								
Marriage	30 Jun 1861	Aston, Warwickshire, England; Parish Church of St Peter and ...		1	1	0		Preferred

Figure 4-1. Alternate birth facts on the Person tab.

Note: An alternate fact doesn't have to include conflicting information. For example, you may have three Address facts for an individual, all of which are correct.

Choosing a Preferred Fact

When you enter multiple facts for the same life event, you'll have to choose which fact is preferred. Typically, this is the fact that is the most accurate or complete. Preferred facts are shown by default in the editing panel, charts, and reports.

1. Go to the **Person** tab on the People workspace and select the appropriate individual.

2. Click the **Facts** button; then click the fact you want to make preferred.

3. In the editing panel click the **Options** button and choose **Preferred** from the drop-down list.

The Preferred column in the Individual & Shared Facts section now shows the fact as preferred.

Tip: You can also set a preferred fact by right-clicking the fact and choosing **Set As Preferred** from the drop-down list.

Making a Fact Private

You may enter facts that you don't want to share with other family members or researchers. If you make a fact private, you can choose whether or not to include it in reports and when you export a tree.

1. Go to the **Person** tab on the People workspace and select the appropriate individual.

2. Click the **Facts** button; then click the fact you want to be private.

3. In the editing panel click the **Options** button and choose **Mark as Private** from the drop-down list.

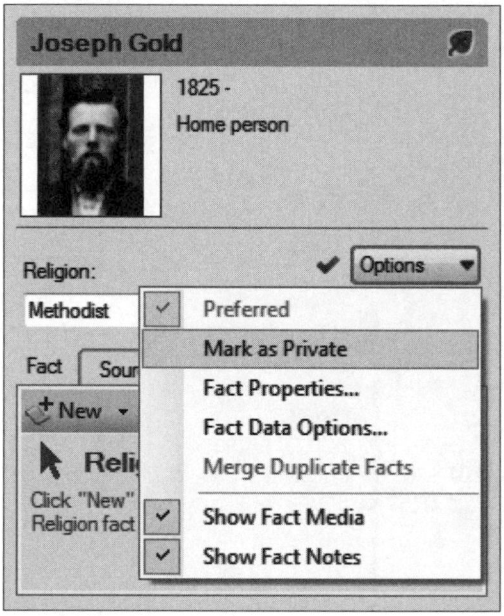

A lock icon will appear next to the private fact in the Individual & Shared Facts section (fig. 4-2).

Individual Facts

Address	1851	Little Ann, Birmingham, England
Baptism	12 Sep 1825	Coventry, Warwickshire, England
Birth	Abt. 1826	Coventry, Warwick, England
Religion	1865	Warwickshire, England; Methodist
Residence	1845	Fillongley, Warwick, England

Figure 4-2. A lock icon indicates that a fact is private.

Adding a Note for an Individual

You may have family stories, legends, or research resources that you want to refer to occasionally. Family Tree Maker lets you enter this type of information in notes—up to 1MB of space, or about 200 printed pages, per note.

Tip: If you are entering notes from another document on your computer, you can "copy and paste" so you don't have to retype existing text.

Entering a Personal Note

Personal notes may be as simple as a physical description or as lengthy as a transcript of an interview with your grandmother.

Note: You should *not* record source information on the Notes tab; if you do, the information won't be included in source reports.

1. Go to the **Person** tab on the People workspace and select the appropriate individual.

2. Click the **Notes** tab at the bottom of the Person tab. Then click the **Person note** button in the Notes toolbar.

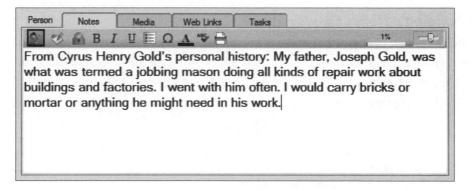

3. Place the cursor in the notes area and enter your text. You can press **Enter** to start a new paragraph.

Entering a Research Note

Sometimes a record or family story will give you clues that can help you learn more about your family. You can create research notes to remind you of the next steps you want to take.

1. Go to the **Person** tab on the People workspace and select the appropriate individual.

2. Click the **Notes** tab at the bottom of the Person tab; then click the **Research note** button in the Notes toolbar.

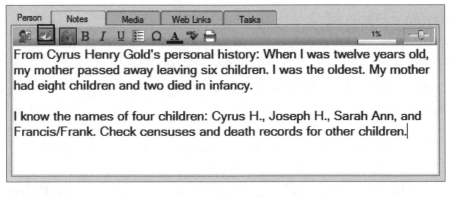

3. Place the cursor in the notes area and enter your text.

Changing a Note's Display Size

You can resize your notes to make the text larger and easier to read or make the text smaller to fit more words on the tab. Simply drag the slider on the right side of the notes toolbar (fig. 4-3). This changes the note's display only; it does not affect how it prints.

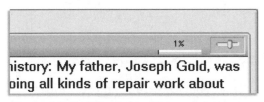

Figure 4-3. A slider on the Notes tab lets you resize the text.

Making a Note Private

You may have information about a relative that you don't want to share with other researchers. If you make a note private, you can choose whether or not to include it in reports and when you export a tree.

After entering a note click the **Toggle private** button. You can tell the note has been marked as private because the lock icon will have a yellow box around it.

Printing a Note

To print a note click the printer button on the Notes toolbar. Select your printing options and click **OK**.

Tip: You can also create a report of any notes you've entered in your tree. Go to the Publish workspace and choose **Person Reports**. Then double-click **Notes Report**.

Adding Web Links for an Individual

If you want to keep track of a website you found about an ancestor or an interesting collection of online maps, you can create a Web link so you can easily access it again.

1. Go to the **Person** tab on the People workspace and select the appropriate individual.

2. Click the **Web Links** tab at the bottom of the Person tab; then click the **New** button in the toolbar.

3. Enter the address for the website.

    Tip: To avoid making a mistake typing the website address, copy the address from your browser and paste it in the field.

4. Enter a name for the link and click **OK**.

Working with Relationships

As you dig deeper into your family history you will discover individuals who marry multiple times, divorces, adoptions, and other special situations. Family Tree Maker can handle all different types of relationships.

Using the Combined Family View

The family group view on the People workspace displays a couple and their mutual children. You can change this view so it displays all children associated with the couple, including children from previous marriages and relationships.

Note: When you display a "blended family" in the family group view, you cannot change the sort order of the children; they will be listed in birth order.

1. Go to the **Tree** tab on the People workspace and select the appropriate family.

2. Click the **Show blended families** button in the family group view.

The combined family group view now displays the children for both individuals. An icon to the left of the child's name indicates whether he or she is the child of the father, the mother, or both parents.

3. To return to the traditional family group view, simply click the **Show blended families** button again.

Viewing an Individual's Family Relationships

You can see all the members of an individual's family at a glance—spouses, children, parents, and siblings.

1. Go to the **Person** tab on the People workspace and select the appropriate individual.

2. Click the **Relationships** button. You can now see parents, siblings, spouses, and children entered for the individual.

Adding Additional Spouses

If an individual in your family has been married more than once, you'll want to enter all additional spouses.

1. Go to the **Tree** tab on the People workspace and select the appropriate individual.

2. In the family group view, click the **Choose spouse** button next to the individual. From the drop-down list, you can view the existing spouse or create a new spouse.

3. Choose **Add Spouse** from the drop-down list.

4. Enter the name of the new spouse and click **OK**. Family Tree Maker displays a new family group view—this time with the new spouse.

5. To view the first spouse again, click the **Choose spouse** button and choose his or her name from the drop-down list.

Choosing a Preferred Spouse

If you enter more than one spouse for an individual, you need to indicate who is the preferred spouse. (Usually this is the spouse whose children are in your direct family line.) The preferred spouse will become the default spouse displayed in the family group view, tree viewer, and charts and reports.

1. Go to the **Tree** tab on the People workspace and select the appropriate individual.

2. Click the **Person** tab; then click the **Relationships** button. You should see two or more names under the Spouses heading.

3. Click the individual you want to be the preferred spouse. Then, in the editing panel, click the **Preferred spouse** checkbox.

Switching Between Spouses

Family Tree Maker displays a person's preferred spouse by default, but you can switch to other spouses when necessary.

1. Go to the **Tree** tab on the People workspace and select the appropriate individual.

2. In the family group view, click the **Choose spouse** button next to the individual. From the drop-down list, choose the spouse you want to view.

Choosing a Type of Relationship for a Couple

You can choose what type of relationship a couple has (e.g., partner, friend, spouse).

1. Go to the **Tree** tab on the People workspace and select the appropriate couple.

2. Click the **Person** tab; then click the **Relationships** button.

3. Click the spouse's name. Then, in the editing panel, choose a relationship type from the **Relationship** drop-down list.

Choosing a Status for a Couple's Relationship

The status of a couple's relationship will default to "Ongoing." If necessary, you can change this status. For example, if a couple gets a divorce, you can indicate this with their relationship status.

1. Go to the **Tree** tab on the People workspace and select the appropriate couple.

2. Click the **Person** tab; then click the **Relationships** button.

3. Click the spouse's name. Then, in the editing panel, choose a status from the **Status** drop-down list.

Choosing a Relationship Between Parents and a Child

You can indicate a child's relationship to each of his or her parents (e.g., biological, adopted, foster).

1. Go to the **Tree** tab on the People workspace and select the appropriate individual.

2. Click the **Person** tab; then click the **Relationships** button.

3. Click the father's or mother's name. Then, in the editing panel, choose a relationship from the **Relationship** drop-down list.

Adding an Unrelated Individual

As you search for family members, you might find a person you suspect is related to you, but you have no proof. You can add this person to your tree without linking them to a specific family. Later on, if you find out that they are related, you can easily link them to the correct family.

1. Click the **People** button on the main toolbar.

2. Click **Person>Add Person>Add Unrelated Person**.

3. Enter the person's name (first, middle, and last). Then choose a gender from the drop-down list and click **OK**.

Viewing a Timeline

Timelines can be a great tool to put the life of your ancestor in context—historical and otherwise. Family Tree Maker has three timeline variations: events in an individual's life; events in the lives of their immediate family (such as birth, marriage, and death); and historical events.

1. Go to the **Person** tab on the People workspace and select the appropriate person. Then click the **Timeline** button.

   A chronological list of events is displayed—along with the person's age at the time of each event.

2. To display events for immediate family members, click the down arrow next to the **Timeline** button and select **Show Family Events**.

Events for the individual are indicated by green markers, and events in his or her family are indicated by pink markers.

3. To display historical events, click the down arrow next to the **Timeline** button and select **Show Historical Events**.

    Historical events are indicated by yellow markers.

Timeline			Facts	Timeline	▾	Relationships	➕ ▾ ✖
Year / Age	Event		Date / Place		Description		
1825	Baptism		12 Sep 1825 Coventry, Warwickshire, England		St. John the Baptist		
1826	Birth		1826 Coventry, Warwickshire, England				
1827 12 mos	Birth (Spouse) Sarah Thompson		1827 Nuneaton, Warwickshire, England				
1830 4	World History Mass Immigration to the Uni		Bet. 1830-1930 Europe, United States, Canada				
1833 7	UK History Slavery Abolition Act of 183		1833 Great Britain				
1834 8	Death (Father) Thomas Gold		Abt. 1834				
1837 11	UK History The Victorian Era		Bet. 1837-1901 Great Britain				
1845 19	UK History The Great Irish Famine		Bet. 1845-1852 Ireland				
1845 19	Marriage Sarah Thompson		27 Jan 1845 Aston, Warwickshire, England		Parish Church of St Peter and St Paul		

4. To learn more about a historical event, click the event. A description appears on the right side of the window.

    Note: Family Tree Maker comes with default historical events that you can edit, delete, and add to. To learn more see "Managing Historical Events" on page 237.

Creating Smart Stories™

Smart Stories is a tool that helps you quickly create stories about individuals and families using the facts, notes, and photos in your tree. And because Smart Stories are linked to the tree, you can edit a fact and the text in your story will be updated automatically. For example, if you find out that Grandpa's birth date is different than you thought, change it in your tree and the story will be updated at the same time.

Family Tree Maker can automatically generate a Smart Story for an individual (fig. 4-4). It will have an image of the person (if you've added a portrait), the individual's immediate family (children, spouses, parents, and siblings), and their life events. You can also create your own Smart Stories, starting with a blank page and adding your own images and text.

You can create Smart Stories on an individual's Media tab, the Media workspace, or the Publish workspace. All stories can be printed, exported, and included in family history books; however, if you upload your tree to Ancestry.com, Smart Stories created on the Publish workspace are considered reports and won't be uploaded.

John W. Bobbitt

John W. Bobbitt was born on 09 Jun 1832 in Kentucky as the first child of Isham Drury Bobbitt and Cyntha Ann Haggard. He had four siblings, namely: Frank, David, Malissa C., and Female. He died on 24 Aug 1909 in Dawson, Richardson, Nebraska. When he was 20, he married Julia Hoyt,daughter of James Hoyt and Maria Hitchcock, on 18 Oct 1852.

Age at Death: (77) His cause of death was Accident; fall resulting in broken hip. 1850 U.S. Census: 1850 in Tazewell County, Illinois, USA 1860 U.S. Census: 1860 in Roberts, Marshall, Illinois, USA 1870 U.S. Census: 1870 in Roberts, Marshall, Illinois, USA Political Office: 1877 in Bell Plain, Marshall, Illinois (Assessor) 1880 U.S. Census: 1880 in Liberty, Richardson, Nebraska, USA He lived in Liberty, Richardson, Nebraska, USA on 11 Jun 1885. He lived in Kenesaw, Adams, Nebraska in 1890. 1900 U.S. Census: 1900 in Van, Woods, Oklahoma He was buried in 1909 in Dawson, Richardson, Nebraska (Heim Cemetery).

John W. Bobbitt and Julia Hoyt had the following children:

1. Seymour Bobbitt was born in Mar 1853 in Illinois.
2. Cornelia O. Bobbitt was born in Mar 1857 in Illinois. She married Hermon P. Shier on 02 Feb 1873 in Varna, Marshall, Illinois.
3. Willis R. Bobbitt was born in Dec 1860 in Illinois.
4. Sarah Eleanor Bobbitt was born about 1863 in Illinois.
5. Francis Marion Bobbitt was born in 1868 in Illinois. He died on 03 Jun 1906 in Topeka, Shawnee, Kansas. He married Julia L. Comstock on 23 Mar 1890 in North Platte, Lincoln, Nebraska.
6. Jessie Julia Bobbitt was born on 03 Mar 1872 in Illinois. She died on 15 Nov 1951 in Los Angeles, Los Angeles, California.
7. Eugene Allen Bobbitt was born in 1877 in Illinois.
8. Female Bobbitt was born on 02 Mar 1872 in Varna, Marshall, Illinois.
9. James Clarence Bobbitt was born on 28 Jul 1858 in Illinois. He died on 02 Jun 1929 in Balko, Beaver, Oklahoma. He married Margaret Rebecca Shanklin on 20 Feb 1882 in Marshall County, Illinois.

Figure 4-4. A Smart Story created by Family Tree Maker.

Creating a Smart Story as a Media Item

1. Select the individual you want to create a Smart Story for.

2. Do one of these options:

    *   Go to the **Person** tab for an individual and click the **Media** tab at the bottom of the window. Click the **New** button and choose **Create New Smart Story** from the drop-down menu.

    *   Go to the Media workspace. Then select **Media>Create a New Smart Story**.

3. If you want Family Tree Maker to generate the story for you, click **Auto-populate Smart Story**. To create your own story, click **Start with blank page**.

4. Click **OK**.

Creating a Smart Story as a Report

1. Go to the **Collection** tab on the Publish workspace. In Publication Types, click **Other**.

2. Double-click the **Smart Story** icon. The editor opens.

    Tip: To access this Smart Story later, go to the Publish workspace and select **Saved Reports**.

Including a Short Biography

1. Place the cursor on the page where you want to add a biography.

2. Click the **Facts** button on the Smart Stories toolbar. Then choose "Personal Biography" from the drop-down list.

3. By default a title, photo, and the individual's immediate family (children, spouses, parents, and siblings) will be included. Deselect the checkboxes for items you don't want.

4. Click the **Insert** button.

Including Facts

1. Place the cursor on the page where you want to add a fact.

2. Click the **Facts** button on the Smart Stories toolbar. Then choose "Facts" from the drop-down list.

3. Select the fact you want to add to your story. Below the fact, you'll see options of how the fact will be entered. You can create a sentence or add specific details.

4. Drag the text to your document or click the **Insert** button.

   Tip: To include the facts, media items, or notes from another person in your tree, click the file folder icon in the top corner and choose a different person.

Including Sources

1. Place the cursor on the page where you want to add a source.

2. Click the **Facts** button on the Smart Stories toolbar. Then choose "Fact Sources" from the drop-down list.

3. Click the fact that has the source you want to add to your story. Below you'll see any associated source citations. If more than one source citation exists for a fact, you can choose it from a drop-down list.

4. Drag the text to your document or click the **Insert** button.

Including Notes

1. Place the cursor on the page where you want to add a note.

2. Click the **Facts** button on the Smart Stories toolbar. Then choose "Notes" from the drop-down list.

3. Drag the text to your document or click the **Insert** button.

Including Images

1. Place the cursor on the page where you want the media item.

2. Click the **Media** button on the Smart Stories toolbar.

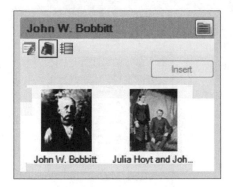

3. Select the media item you want to use.

4. Drag the image to your document or click the **Insert** button.

Creating Timelines

You can use facts in a person's life and historical events to create a timeline.

1. Place the cursor on the page where you want to add an event.

2. Click the **Timeline** button on the Smart Stories toolbar. Then choose an event type from the drop-down list.

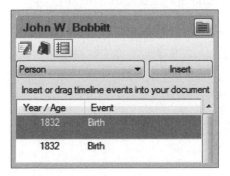

3. Click the event you want to add to your story. Below the event you'll see options of how the event will be entered. You can create a sentence or add specific details.

4. Drag the text to your document or click the **Insert** button.

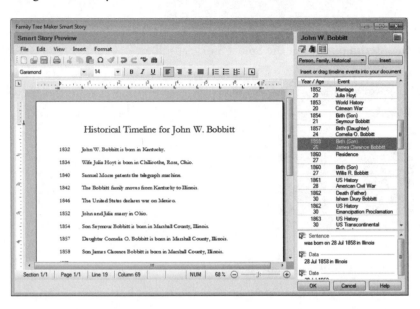

Editing Smart Stories Text

Smart Stories pulls text directly from your tree. That means you don't have to worry about continually redoing your story; if information in your tree changes, your story will be updated automatically.

You can also edit text in Smart Stories. But, be aware that the text will no longer be linked to your tree and will not be updated automatically.

1. Move the cursor over the text you want to add, edit, or delete. You can identify which text is linked to your tree because it will be highlighted.

> John W. Bobbitt was born on 09 Jun 1832 in Kentucky as the first child of Isham Drury Bobbitt and Cyntha Ann Haggard. He had four siblings, namely: Frank, David, Malissa C., and Female. He died on 24 Aug 1909 in Dawson, Richardson, Nebraska. When he was 20, he married Julia Hoyt, daughter of James Hoyt and Maria Hitchcock, on 18 Oct 1852.

2. Double-click the text block. A message asks whether you want to edit the text.

3. Click **Yes**.

Chapter Five
Documenting Your Research

Documenting sources—recording where you discovered a fact—is one of the most important aspects of your research. Sources are valuable for many reasons. When you cite a source, you are proving to others which records you based your facts on; if you eventually share your research with your family or other researchers, your family history may be judged for accuracy based on your sources. If your sources are detailed and correct, others will be able to follow your research footsteps.

Each time you add information to your tree, you'll want to create a source and source citation that describe where you found the info. For example, if you find your father's birthplace on his World War I draft card, you'll create a source for the record when you add his birth date and birthplace.

Understanding Sources and Source Citations

If you're new to family history, you may not be familiar with sources and source citations. This section gives an explanation of each and also shows you some examples.

- A source is the unchanging facts about an item; for example, the author, title, and publication information for a book.

- Source citations are individual details that explain where you found a fact, such as the page number in a book.

To help you understand how sources and source citations work together, let's look at an example from the 1930 United States Federal Census. First, you would create a source for the census that includes information like this:

- A title—1930 United States Federal Census

- Where you located the source—www.ancestry.com

- Publishing details—Bureau of the Census. Washington, D.C.: National Archives and Records Administration, 1930.

As you can see, these details about the 1930 census won't change regardless of who or what you find in the records. However, because you'll find families and individuals in different locations throughout the census, each census fact will need its own source citation. A source citation for an individual in the 1930 census might include this information:

- Source—1930 United States Federal Census

- Source citation—Harold Reed household, Santa Clara Township, Santa Clara County, California. Roll: 219; Page: 14A; Enumeration district: 110.

A source citation for a different individual in the 1930 census might look like this. (Notice the source is the same as the previous example.)

- Source—1930 United States Federal Census

- Source citation—Michael Reed household, Kokomo Township, Beaver County, Oklahoma. Roll: 1892; Page: 5B; Enumeration district: 26.

Both individuals can be found in the 1930 census (the source), but the source citation for each individual has changed because the individuals were recorded in different places in the source.

Creating Sources

Family Tree Maker lets you create sources in two ways: using templates or a basic format. Source templates are useful because you don't have to guess which details need to be entered. Choose the type of source you're creating (for example an obituary) and Family Tree Maker displays the relevant fields. If you don't want to use a template (for example, because you have your own system of citation or you can't find a matching template), you can create a source by completing the standard fields (author, title, and publisher) in the basic source format.

Adding a Source for a Fact

You will usually add a source as you create a source citation for a fact or event you are entering in your tree. This section focuses on adding a source while entering facts on the Family tab in the People workspace.

Note: You need to create only one source for each item; you can use a source for as many source citations as necessary.

1. Go to the **Tree** tab on the People workspace.

2. In the editing panel click the **New source citation** button next to the fact you want to add a source to. Then choose **Add New Source Citation** from the drop-down list.

3. The Add Source Citation window opens. To create a source using a template, continue with "Creating a Source from a Template." To create a basic source, continue with "Creating a Source Using the Basic Format."

Using Source Templates

Family Tree Maker has more than 170 templates to help you source everything from homemade samplers and online databases to vital records. These source templates are based on the QuickCheck models used in Elizabeth Shown Mills's book *Evidence Explained*—the premier reference for citing genealogy sources.

Creating a Source from a Template

Using a source template is simple. To determine which template you should use, enter keywords and choose from a list of suggestions, or view a list of all available templates and choose the one that fits best.

To choose a template using keywords

1. Access the Add Source Citation window and click **New**. (For help see "Adding a Source for a Fact.")

2. Enter a keyword in the **Source template** field and choose a template from the list. To narrow the list, enter multiple keywords. For example, "property" brings up eleven results, while "property grant" brings up one result.

3. The fields that appear now reflect the template you've chosen. Complete these fields as necessary and click **OK**.

You can now add a source citation for the fact (see page 68).

To choose a template from a list

1. Access the Add Source Citation window and click **New**. (If you need help see "Adding a Source for a Fact.") The Add Source window opens.

2. Click **More**.

3. In Source group choose the group that most closely matches the item you're sourcing. The categories list changes to reflect the selected group.

4. Choose the appropriate category from the **Category** drop-down list. The templates list changes to reflect the selected source group and category.

5. Choose a template from the **Template** drop-down list. A description of the template is displayed beneath its title.

6. Click **OK** to return to the Add Source window; the fields that appear now reflect the template you've chosen. Complete these fields as necessary and click **OK**. You can now add a source citation for the fact (see page 68).

Creating a Source Using the Basic Format

If you don't want to use a source template, you can create a source by simply completing some standard fields (such as author, title, and publisher) in the basic source format.

1. Access the Add Source Citation window and click **New**. (If you need help see "Adding a Source for a Fact.") The Add Source window opens.

2. Complete the source fields as necessary:

   - **Title.** Enter the title of the source exactly as it appears in the source.

   - **Author.** Enter the author or originator's name.

   - **Publisher name.** Enter the name of the publishing company.

- **Publisher location.** Enter the place of publication (for example, London, England).

- **Publish date.** Enter the copyright date for the source (usually only a year).

- **Source repository.** Create a new repository or choose one from the drop-down list.

  A repository is the location where an original source exists. This could be a library, county courthouse, or cousin's home. To create a repository, click **New**. Then enter the name, address, email, and phone number for the location.

- **Call number.** Enter a call number, if one exists.

  The call number is the number assigned to the source at the repository. It could be a microfilm number, a Dewey Decimal system number, or some other numbering system unique to a particular library or archive.

- **Comments.** Enter any comments about the source and the information found in it. This information will not print on your reports; it is for your personal reference. You might include a description of the item or information about its legibility.

3. Click **OK**. You can now add a source citation for the fact (see page 68).

Creating Source Citations

After you create a source, you're ready to identify where in the source you found information by creating a source citation. Family Tree Maker lets you create source citations in a variety of ways; you'll need to decide which method is most effective for you.

Note: You can have more than one source citation for the same fact. For example, you might find an immigration date for your great-grandmother on a naturalization record and a census record. You should make source citations for both records.

Adding a New Source Citation

Each time you add a fact to your tree, you should take a minute to document where you discovered the information, whether it's a book in a library or a record you found online. When you create a new source citation, you'll link it to a source and add any additional identifying information such as page or volume number.

1. Access the Add Source Citation window. (If you need help see "Adding a Source for a Fact.")

2. Change the citation as necessary:

```
┌─────────────────────────────────────────────────────────────────────┐
│ Add Source Citation For Marriage of Julia Hoyt                    [x] │
├─────────────────────────────────────────────────────────────────────┤
│ ┌Source┐ Reference Note │ Media │ Notes                               │
│                                                                       │
│ Source title:   Hoyt, David D., A Genealogical History of the Hoyt, Hai ▼  [ New... ]  [ Edit... ] │
│                                                                       │
│ Repository:     Family History Library                                │
│ Citation detail: Page 566. Family of James Hoyt.                      │
│                                                                       │
│ Citation text:  (6008) Julia b. Sept. 6. 1834 in Chillicothe, Ohio: m. John W. Bobbitt. Oct. 18. 1852; res. │
│                 Robertstown, Marshall Co. Illinois                    │
│                                                                       │
│ Web address:    Enter a web address for the source.                   │
│                                                                       │
│                 ┌Include in reference note──────────┐                 │
│                 │ ☑ Citation text    ☑ Web address  │                 │
│                 └───────────────────────────────────┘                 │
│                                                                       │
│ [ Copy ]                       [ OK ]   [ Cancel ]   [ Help ]         │
└─────────────────────────────────────────────────────────────────────┘
```

- **Source title.** From the drop-down list, choose the source of the information.

- **Citation detail.** Enter details about where you found the information in the source, such as the page number.

- **Citation text.** Enter any additional information. For example, you might enter a quote from a book or add a paraphrased summary of the source text.

- **Web address.** For online sources, enter the URL where the information was found.

- **Include in reference note.** Click the **Citation text** checkbox to include text in the Citation text field in printed reference notes. Click the **Web address** checkbox to include the source's URL in printed reference notes. (The source title and citation detail are always included in reference notes.)

You can include a media item or note as part of a source citation. For instructions see "Attaching a Media Item to a Source Citation" and "Adding a Note to a Source Citation."

3. Click **OK**.

Linking a Fact to an Existing Source Citation

If you've already created a citation for a source, such as a death certificate, you don't have to create another source citation for each fact or individual in the source. For example, if you find your grandparents' names and birthplaces in your aunt's death certificate, you don't have to create a new source citation for the death certificate; you can simply link these facts to the citation you already created.

1. Go to the **Person** tab on the People workspace and select the appropriate individual.

2. Click the **Facts** button. Then click the fact you want to add a source citation to.

3. On the **Sources** tab, click the **New** button and choose **Use Existing Source Citation** from the drop-down list.

The Find Source Citation window opens.

4. Click the citation you want to link to from the list.

5. Click **Link to Citation**. The citation information now appears on the Sources tab.

Copying and Updating a Source Citation

If you need to create a source citation that is similar to one already in your tree, don't make a new citation. Simply copy the old one and update details as necessary (such as a page number). For example, if several family members are in the same city directory for Cleveland, Ohio, you can create a source citation for one family, then copy and update the source citation for other families in the directory.

1. Go to the **Person** tab on the People workspace and select the appropriate individual.

2. Click the **Facts** button. Then click the fact that you want to add a source citation to.

3. On the **Sources** tab, click the **New** button and choose **Use Existing Source Citation** from the drop-down list. The Find Source Citation window opens.

4. Click the citation you want to copy from the list.

5. Click **Create New Copy**. A citation link appears on the Sources tab on the Person page.

Now you can edit the citation without affecting the original.

6. Double-click the source citation to open it in an editing window. Then make any necessary changes and click **OK**.

Attaching a Media Item to a Source Citation

If you have an image or recording of a source, you can link it to a source citation. For example, you might have a scan of a marriage certificate or census record that you want to add to the source citation.

1. Click the **Media** tab in a source citation.

2. Do one of these options:

   - If the media item is already in your tree, click **Link to Existing Media**. Click the item you want then click **OK**.

   - To add a media item, click **Attach New Media**. Use the file management window to navigate to the media item. Then click **Open**.

3. Click **OK**.

Adding a Note to a Source Citation

You can use the Notes tab for additional information you have about a source that you weren't able to include elsewhere. For example, you can enter a note about how you discovered a source or where the source is located.

1. Click the **Notes** tab in a source citation.

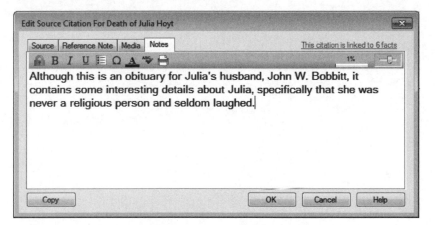

2. Enter a note and click **OK**.

Chapter Six
Including Media Items

As you gather names, dates, and facts, you'll realize that these tell only part of your family's story. In order to really bring your ancestors to life, you'll want to illustrate your family history with photographs, important documents, and video and sound clips.

Family Tree Maker helps you organize your multimedia items in one central location. You can link media items to specific individuals; record important notes and information about the items; use the images in family tree charts; and more.

What Media Items Can I Add to My Tree?

Photographs are usually the first thing that comes to mind when you want to illustrate your family history. But don't limit yourself; many personal objects can be scanned or photographed. Here are some items you might want to add to your tree:

- Important records, such as birth and marriage certificates, censuses, passports, diplomas, obituaries, and family Bibles.

- Photographs of heirlooms or items with sentimental value, such as jewelry, medals, artwork, quilts, christening outfits, and furniture.

- Images of ancestral houses and hometowns, churches, maps, cemeteries, and headstones.

- Family documents, such as letters, funeral books, diaries, Christmas cards, and newspaper and magazine articles.

- Audio clips of oral histories and family stories.

Adding Media Items

If you have a baby picture of your grandma or a photo of your grandpa's military uniform, you'll want to add it to your tree. You can add photos, audio files, and videos from your computer or you can scan documents directly into Family Tree Maker.

Adding a Media Item for an Individual

1. Go to the **Person** tab on the People workspace and select the appropriate individual.

2. Click the **Media** tab at the bottom of the window.

3. Click the **New** button and choose **Add New Media** from the drop-down list.

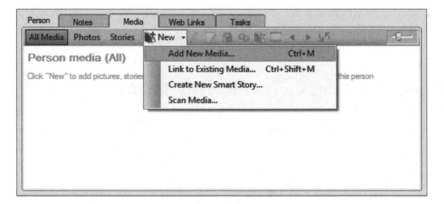

Note: When you add a media item to Family Tree Maker, the original file is not moved from its location on your computer.

4. Use the file management window to navigate to the media item you want to add to your tree. Then click **Open**.

Tip: You can select multiple media items by clicking on each file while pressing the CTRL key.

A message asks whether you want to link the file(s) to your tree or create a copy of the file(s).

5. Click **Copy this file** to create an additional copy of the file in a Family Tree Maker media folder, or click **Link to this file** to link to the file on your computer only.

Tip: Make copies of your media items if you want all your heritage photos and other media items saved in one central location on your computer. This makes them easier to find and easier to back up.

6. Click the checkbox for the category you want this item to belong to; you can select multiple categories. (For more information see "Media Categories.")

7. Click **OK**. The item is added to the individual's Media tab.

Scanning an Image into Your Tree

If you have images you'd like to add to your tree that aren't already on your computer, you can scan them directly into your tree.

When you scan an image, you'll choose the resolution in which the item will be saved. The higher the resolution, or DPI (dots per inch), the sharper your image—and the larger the file size that will be created. If you plan on viewing your images online or sharing them via email, scan images at a lower resolution such as 72 to 150 DPI; if you want to print images in charts and reports, use a higher resolution such as 200 to 300 DPI.

1. Make sure your scanner is connected to your computer and turned on.

2. Go to the Media workspace and choose **Media>Scan Media**. Family Tree Maker automatically searches for connected scanners.

3. Change any settings and click **Scan**. The image is added to the Media workspace.

Changing the Display of an Image

When you're viewing a photo, you can change the display of the image by rotating the image or zooming in and out on the image.

Go to the **Collection** tab on the Media workspace. Double-click a photo or click the image and click the **Detail** tab.

Use these buttons in the image toolbar to change the display:

 Click the **Rotate right** button to move the image clockwise; click the **Rotate left** button to move the image counterclockwise.

 Click the **Magnifier** button to turn the cursor into a magnifying glass when viewing the image.

 Click the **Size to fit** button to display the entire image in the current window.

Click the **Actual size** button to show the actual size of the image. You can also choose a specific percentage from the **Fit Image** drop-down list.

Entering Details for a Media Item

After you add a media item, it's a good idea to enter details about it such as a caption, date, and description.

1. Go to the **Collection** tab on the Media workspace. Double-click a media item, or click the image and click the **Detail** tab.

2. Change the image's details as necessary:

    -   **Caption.** Enter a brief title for the item.

    -   **Date.** Enter a date for the item. (Typically this is the date the item was created.)

    -   **Description.** Describe the media item in detail. For photos you can enter the names of individuals or info about the location depicted; for heirlooms you may want to explain what the item is and its significance to your family.

3. Click the **Private** checkbox to keep this media item from being exported or uploaded to your online Ancestry tree.

4. To assign a category to the item, click the **Edit** button next to the **Categories** field. Mark the checkbox for the category you want this item to belong to; you can select multiple categories. Click **OK** when you're finished.

   Tip: You can click the File name and location link to open the Media folder and view the actual media item.

Entering a Note About a Media Item

If you have details that won't fit in a media item's description, you can enter it in the item's notes. For example, a photo of your grandmother in her graduation robes may include notes about her college education and how you found the image.

1. Go to the **Collection** tab on the Media workspace. Double-click the media item you want to add a note to, or click the image and click the **Detail** tab.

2. Click the **Notes** tab at the bottom of the window and enter the information.

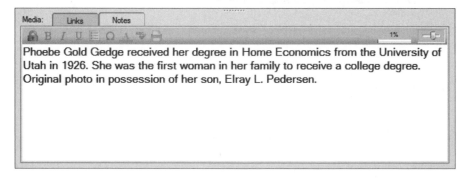

Note: For more information about using notes, see "Adding a Note for an Individual" on page 44.

Adding a Portrait for an Individual

If you want to display a photo of an individual in charts, reports, and the People workspace, you'll need to add a portrait for them.

1. Click the **People** button on the main toolbar. Make sure the individual you want to add a portrait to is the focus of the Tree tab or Person tab.

2. In the editing panel right-click the person silhouette and do one of these options.

   • If the photo is already in your tree, click **Link to Existing Picture**. A media item window opens. Click the image you want then click **OK**.

   • If you're adding a new image, click **Add New Picture**. Use the file management window to navigate to the image. Then click **Open**.

Linking a Media Item to Multiple Individuals

You may have a family photo that includes several individuals in your tree. You don't have to add the picture to each individual; simply add it once to the Media workspace, then link it to the necessary individuals. You can also link media items to specific facts. For example, if you have a photograph of the ship on which your grandparents immigrated to America, you can link the picture to your grandparents and their immigration fact.

1. Go to the **Collection** tab on the Media workspace. Then double-click the item you want to link to multiple individuals, or click the item and click the **Detail** tab.

2. At the bottom of the Detail tab, you'll see a Links tab. Click the **New** button and choose **Link to Person**.

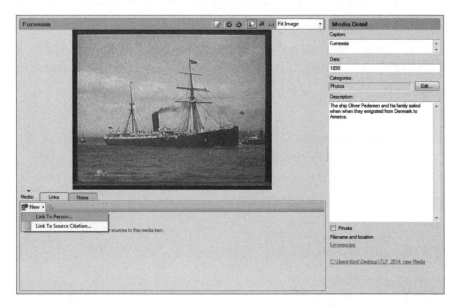

3. In the **Name** column, click the name of the individual you want to link the media item to.

4. Do one of these options:

    - To link the item to a person, click **Link to person only**. (You can link to one person at a time.)

    - To link the item to a specific fact (such as birth), click **Link to person's fact**. Then click the fact in the list below.

5. Click **OK**.

    Tip: If you mistakenly link a media item to an individual, you can unlink it on the Detail tab. Click the appropriate individual and then click the broken link icon in the toolbar.

Managing Media Items

Occasionally you might need to do some organizational tasks for your media items such as change file names or assign categories.

Opening a Media Item from Family Tree Maker

If you need to edit an image or read a document in your tree, you can open it in its default program without leaving Family Tree Maker.

Go to the **Collection** tab on the Media workspace. Double-click a media item or click the image and click the **Detail** tab. Then click the **Open file** button in the image toolbar. The media item opens in the file's default program. If you edit the media item and save your changes, the modified file will be linked to Family Tree Maker.

Changing a Media Item's File Name

Family Tree Maker lets you change a media item's file name on your computer. This can be useful if you've imported a tree and its media files have generic names; you can use Family Tree Maker to change these file names to something more identifiable.

1. Go to the **Collection** tab on the Media workspace. Right-click a media item and choose **Rename Media File** from the drop-down list, or click a media item and choose **Media>Rename Media File**.

2. Enter the new name for the file and click **OK**.

Arranging an Individual's Media Items

When you add media items for an individual, they are arranged in alphabetical order (by caption). You can change the order in which they appear on the individual's Media tab. For example, you may want to display the pictures by date.

1. Go to the **Person** tab on the People workspace and select the appropriate individual.

2. Click the **Media** tab at the bottom of the window. The tab shows thumbnails of any media items you've linked to this individual.

Use these buttons in the media toolbar to change the display order:

 Click the item you want to move. Then click the **Move Media Forward** and **Move Media Backward** buttons to rearrange the media items. The items will remain in the order you've chosen.

 Click the **Auto Sort Media** button to arrange the media items alphabetically (by caption).

Media Categories

As you add each media item to your tree, you can assign it to categories. These categories make your media items easier to search for, sort, and view.

Creating a Category

You can use the default categories, modify them, or create your own. If you decide to create your own categories, you might want to set up a system before you add your media items. For example, you may want to have event categories (e.g., Weddings, Birthdays, Travel) or categories based on item types (e.g., Photos—Portraits, Movies—Holidays).

1. Go to the **Collection** tab on the Media workspace. In the media editing panel, click the **Edit** button.

2. Click the **Add** button.

3. Enter a name for the category and click **OK**.

Assigning a Category to Multiple Items

Family Tree Maker lets you assign categories to a group of items at the same time.

1. Go to the **Collection** tab on the Media workspace.

2. Select the media items you want to assign a category to. You can select multiple media items by clicking on each file while pressing the **CTRL** key.

3. Click **Media>Categorize Media**.

4. From the drop-down list, you can choose each media item one by one or all selected items.

5. Click the checkboxes for the categories you want to assign the items and click **OK**.

Printing a Media Item

1. Go to the **Collection** tab on the Media workspace and click the item you want to print.

2. Click the **Print** button on the main toolbar and choose **Print Media Item** from the drop-down list.

3. When prompted choose a printer, select the number of copies, and choose a page range.

4. Click **Print**.

Creating a Slide Show

You can create a slide show of pictures you've included in your tree—and even include a sound track. You can view your completed slide shows using *Windows Media Player*.

1. Click the **Media** button on the main toolbar. Click **Media**>**Create Slide Show**.

Tip: You can create a slide show for a specific individual by clicking the **Create slide show** button on the individual's Media tab.

2. Change the slide show options as necessary:

    - **Title.** Enter a name for the slide show. (This will be the item's file name on your computer also.)

    - **Images to include.** To include pictures from a specific category, choose the category name from the drop-down list. Click the **Include relationship media** checkbox to include images linked to relationships; click the **Include fact media** checkbox to include images linked to facts.

- **Image caption.** Choose what text is displayed for images. Click **None** to hide captions; click **Use Captions Only** to display image captions; click **Use Filenames Only** to display file names; click **Use Captions or Filenames** to display captions (if no caption has been entered, the file name will be displayed).

  Click the **Font** button to choose a font style, size, and color for captions and file names used in the slide show.

- **Movie size.** Choose the display size of the slide show from the drop-down list.

  Note: The larger the movie, the more memory required.

- **Movie quality.** Choose the display quality of the slide show from the drop-down list.

  Note: The better quality the movie, the more memory required.

- **Transition delay.** Choose the number of seconds an image is displayed.

- **Sound track.** To add music to the slide show, click the **Browse** button and locate the MP3 or Windows Media Audio (.wma) file you'd like to use.

3. Click **Next**. Now you can change the order in which images appear or delete images you don't want.

4. Click **Next**. A preview window opens.

5. Do one of these options:

- To save the slide show to your tree, click **Add slide show to the media collection**.

- To view the finished slide show in *Windows Media Player*, click **Launch slide show in Windows Media Player**.

6. Click **Finish**. A message asks whether you want to save the file to your tree or save the file to another location.

7. Click **Save this file to the media folder** to save the slide show to the Family Tree Maker media folder, or click **Save the slide show in another location** to choose a location.

8. Click the checkbox for the category you want this item to belong to; you can select multiple categories.

9. Click **OK**.

Chapter Seven
Using Maps

As you gather the names and dates of important events in your ancestors' lives, you'll also record the locations where these events took place—the towns, cities, and countries that shaped their daily lives.

Often, these places exist only as names in a report or on a pedigree chart. Family Tree Maker brings these ancestral homelands to life by letting you virtually visit each place in your tree. For example, you can see satellite images and maps of the town in Denmark where your grandfather was born, the apartment in Chicago where your great-grandparents lived, or even the lake where you went swimming with your cousins every summer.

Each time you enter a location for a fact or event, Family Tree Maker adds it to a "master list" of locations. To view this master list, simply go to the Places workspace. You can then view maps and satellite images of a location, identify individuals in your tree who are associated with certain locations, and more.

Viewing a Map

The interactive online maps in Family Tree Maker are easy to navigate using a few simple tools. You can zoom in and out on the map, change the type of map you're viewing, and more.

Note: You must be connected to the Internet to view these maps.

1. Click the **Places** button on the main toolbar. To access a map, click a location in the **Places** panel.

   A road map (the default view) appears in the display area, the location centered on the map and marked with a red pushpin. In the top, left-hand corner of the map are tools, which remain on the map regardless of which view you're looking at.

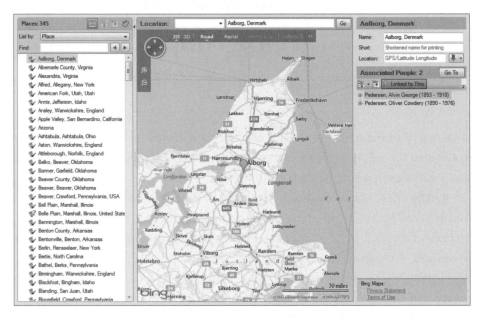

To change the type of map you're viewing, simply click the appropriate view in the map tools.

Microsoft® Bing™ Maps

Family Tree Maker has partnered with Microsoft *Bing Maps* to let you access some of the most exciting technology available today. *Bing Maps* takes you beyond typical road maps by combining them with satellite and aerial imagery to let you experience the world as it looks today.

As you visit different locations, you'll notice that the level of detail for each town, region, or country varies. In some areas you can zoom in close enough to see cars, rooftops, and street intersections; in other areas your view will disappear when you get within a mile of the location. Fortunately, *Bing Maps* is updated regularly and regions that may not have many images now will in the future. The most detailed views are of the United States, the United Kingdom, Canada, and Australia.

Note: This feature is subject to change without notice.

2. Click **Aerial** to view a satellite image of the location.

3. In the aerial view click **Labels** to switch between the aerial view and a combination of the road and aerial views.

4. Click **Road** to display the street map again.

5. To see a street-level view of the location, click **Bird's eye**. Click the points of the compass on the map tools to change the direction you are viewing.

Note: The bird's-eye view is available only for certain parts of the world.

6. Click **3D** to change the map from two dimensions to three. You can use this mode in road and aerial views. (The first time you view 3-D maps you'll be prompted to download plug-in software from Microsoft. You can't view 3-D maps without it.)

To rotate the image, press the **CTRL** key and hold down the left mouse button as you move the mouse. Maneuvering in 3-D can be tricky, so it might take some practice before you're able to view the map as you'd like.

Tip: You can also change the 3-D view by clicking the **Rotate camera** and **Tilt** buttons.

Moving Around a Map

You can quickly change the part of the map you're viewing by "dragging" it. Move the cursor over the map. When the cursor changes to a hand icon, click and hold down either mouse key. Now drag the map wherever you want.

Zooming In and Out on a Map

You can use the plus and minus buttons on the map tools to zoom in and out on the displayed map.

1. Click the plus sign (+) to magnify the map one level at a time; click the button and hold the mouse button to rapidly zoom in on the map.

2. Click the minus sign (-) to minimize the map one level at a time; click the button and hold the mouse button to rapidly zoom out on the map.

Finding Places of Interest

Family Tree Maker helps you search for places of interest such as libraries and cemeteries near important places in your family history. If you're planning a research trip, you can use the maps to view all the cemeteries and churches in your ancestor's hometown. You can also type in other attractions and sights—try searching for "hotel", "park", or even "gas station".

1. Click the **Places** button on the main toolbar.

2. If you've already entered the location in your tree, click its name in the **Places** panel; otherwise, enter the location's name in the blank field above the map on the right.

3. Choose a location type (such as cemeteries) from the drop-down list and click **Go**. (You can also type your own search term in the Location field.) Blue pushpins appear for each item that matches your search.

4. Move the mouse over a pushpin to see a name and address for the location (if available).

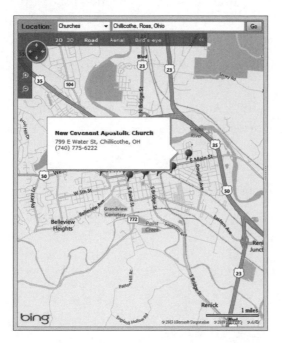

Printing a Map

You can print maps directly from the software, whether it's an aerial shot of your ancestor's farm or the migration path your great-grandfather took across the country.

Note: You can print two- and three-dimensional maps but not bird's-eye views.

1. Access the map you want to print on the Places workspace. The display window shows what part of the map will be printed. You may need to resize the workspace to display more of the map.

2. In the main toolbar click the **Print** button and choose **Print Map** from the drop-down list. The Print window opens.

3. When prompted choose a printer, select the number of copies, and choose a page range.

4. Click **Print**.

Viewing Locations in Groups

On the Places workspace you can view locations in an alphabetical list or grouped together by country, county, city, and so on. If you have hundreds of places in your tree, groups make it easier to quickly find the one you're interested in. An added benefit is that you can see all people who are associated with a specific country or city with one click.

Note: To make sure locations are grouped together correctly, you'll need to resolve any place name errors. For help, see "Standardizing Locations" on page 252.

1. Click the **Places** button on the main toolbar.

2. In the Places panel click the groups button.

3. To see all places within a group, click the arrow button next to it.

Viewing People and Facts Linked to a Location

Family Tree Maker lets you view all the events that took place at a certain location and the people associated with each event.

1. Click the **Places** button on the main toolbar.

2. Click a location in the **Places** panel.

Tip: If you're viewing locations in groups, click on a country, state, or city to see all the events for that group. Click the **Link to This** button to view people and events for the selected location; click the **Linked to All** button to view all people and events in the group.

On the right side of the window, you'll see the selected location and the individuals who have life events associated with it.

3. Do one of these options:

    •   To see the event that occurred at this location for a specific person, click the plus sign (+).

    •   To see the events that occurred at this location for all individuals, click the **Expand all items** button on the toolbar and choose **Expand all**. (Click the **Collapse all items** button to close all the events.)

    •   If you want location events to always appear in the panel, click the **Expand all items** button on the toolbar and choose **Expand All on Load**.

Creating Migration Maps

Maps can be extremely useful when tracing an ancestor. You can see at a glance all the locations that are connected with a specific individual or family, track migration patterns, and maybe discover where to locate more records.

Creating a Migration Map for an Individual

1. Click the **Places** button on the main toolbar. In the Places panel choose "Person" from the **List by** drop-down list.

2. Click the individual whose migration map you want to see. A map appears in the display area; the individual's birthplace is indicated by a green marker and a death place by a red marker.

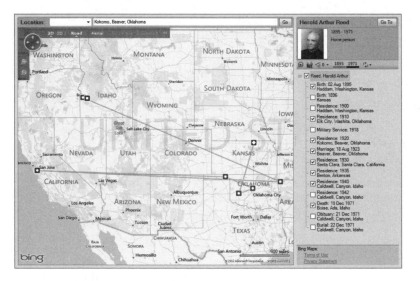

To the right of the map is every fact you've entered for an individual—and its location.

3. Click the checkbox next to a fact to include its location in the map.

4. Mouse over a marker to see the location's name and fact associated with it.

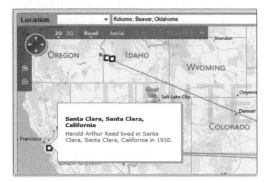

Creating a Migration Map for a Family

1. Click the **Places** button on the main toolbar. In the Places panel choose "Person" from the **List by** drop-down list and click an individual.

2. To view the locations associated with the individual's immediate family (parents, siblings, spouse, and children), click the **Include immediate family** button in the mapping toolbar.

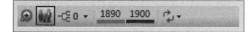

3. Click any individual's name to the right of the map to highlight his or her life events on the map. The migration path for the individual is indicated by a thick line.

   Tip: You can change the color of a migration path by clicking the line color buttons in the mapping toolbar.

4. To view locations associated with an individual's ancestors (up to four generations), click the **Ancestor generations** button in the mapping toolbar and choose the number of generations from the drop-down.

   A map appears in the display area: birthplaces are indicated by green markers and death places by red markers; the migration path for each individual is indicated by a colored line.

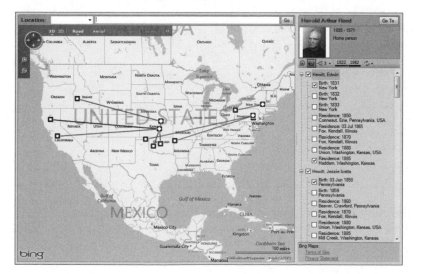

Entering GPS Coordinates

Although the online maps are able to recognize most places, there are times when it won't be able to identify a location. Perhaps your grandma is buried in a rural cemetery or census records show your family in a township that no longer exists. You can set a location's exact position using GPS (Global Positioning System) coordinates.

1. Click the **Places** button on the main toolbar. In the Places panel click the name of the location to which you want to add GPS coordinates.

2. Place your cursor in the **Location** field then click the **Location calculator** button that appears.

   The Location Calculator opens. You can enter the coordinates in degrees:minutes:seconds, degrees:decimal minutes, or decimal degrees.

3. Enter the coordinates for the location and click **OK**.

Entering a Display Name for a Location

Recording locations in a complete and consistent manner is an important part of creating a quality family history. Unfortunately, long location names can clutter your reports and charts. To avoid this problem, you can enter your own shortened or abbreviated display names. For example, instead using Heidelberg, Baden-Württemberg, Germany, for a birthplace, you can enter Heidelberg, Germany, as the display name.

1. Click the **Places** button on the main toolbar. In the Places panel choose "Place" from the **List by** drop-down list.

2. Click the name of the location you want to change.

3. Enter a display name in the **Short** field.

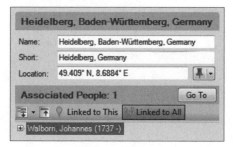

Chapter Eight
Researching Your Tree Online

As you enter stories and facts, you'll probably notice that more information about your family is waiting to be discovered—perhaps it's the burial location of your grandfather or the wedding certificate for your aunt and uncle. Family Tree Maker can help you fill in these gaps in your research with Ancestry Hints—behind-the-scenes searches of Ancestry.com.

You can also search for information on RootsWeb.com, Genealogy.com, or any of your favorite websites. If you find info that matches a family member, you can quickly add it to your tree—without leaving Family Tree Maker.

Ancestry Hints

Family Tree Maker automatically searches Ancestry.com looking for information that matches people in your tree. When a possible match is found, a green leaf or "hint" appears next to an individual in the tree viewer and editing panel on the People workspace (fig. 8-1).

You can view the results when it's convenient, and if the information is relevant, you can add it to your tree.

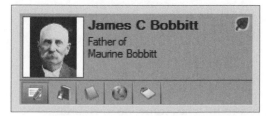

Figure 8-1. Ancestry Hints waiting to be viewed.

Note: If you don't want Family Tree Maker to automatically search Ancestry.com when you're connected to the Internet, you can turn off this feature. You can also exclude Ancestry Member Trees from hints. To change these preferences, click **Tools>Options**.

Viewing Hints

If Family Tree Maker finds records or trees on Ancestry.com that might match an individual in your tree, you'll see a green leaf next to the person on the People workspace. Move the mouse over the leaf icon to see the number of records and trees that were found.

Note: To view Ancestry Hints you must register your copy of Family Tree Maker and have an Internet connection. To view the actual records and images, you must have a subscription to Ancestry.com.

1. Go to the **Tree** tab on the People workspace. In the tree viewer or editing panel, click the green leaf icon.

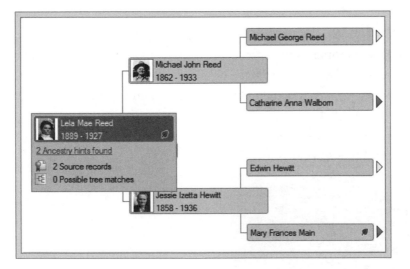

2. Click a hint that interests you. If the record matches someone in your family, you can add it to your tree. (For instructions see "Adding Ancestry.com Records to a Tree.") If the record does not match anyone in your tree, you can ignore it. (For instructions see the next task, "Ignoring Hints.")

Ignoring Hints

If a hint is not relevant to someone in your tree, you can ignore it so it won't appear in your list of hints again.

1. Access the Ancestry Hints for an individual.

2. On the Possible Matches page, click the hint you want to ignore.

3. On the Search Result Detail toolbar, click the **Ignore record** button (a circle with a diagonal line through it). The Ignore record button changes to yellow to show that the hint is being ignored.

Viewing Ignored Hints

If you've chosen to ignore specific Ancestry Hints for an individual, you can still view them at a later time.

1. Click the **Web Search** button on the main toolbar. Using the mini pedigree tree or Index of Individuals button, choose the individual whose hints you'd like to view.

2. Click **Search>View Ignored Records**. (If this individual has no ignored hints, click **OK** and choose another individual.)

3. To take the hint off the Ignore list, click the **Ignore record** button (a circle with a diagonal line through it).

What Can I Find on Ancestry.com?

Ancestry.com is the world's largest online family history resource with more than 11 billion historical records—and more being added all the time. Here's a sample of the wealth of information available on Ancestry:

- A complete U.S. census collection (1790–1940). You'll also find census records for Canada and the UK.
- Immigration records and passenger lists from 1820 to 1960.
- More than 60 million African American records, including slave narratives, censuses, and U.S. Colored Troops service records.
- Birth, marriage, and death records.
- Almost 200 million military records from the 1600s to the Vietnam War.
- Historical newspapers spanning the 1700s through 2013.
- More than 20,000 local histories, memoirs, journals, and biographies.
- Thousands of photos from the Library of Congress, maps beginning in the 1500s, and historical photographs dating back to the mid-1800s.
- Almost 47 million family trees from all over the world—created by researchers just like you. Within these trees you'll find 205 million photographs, scanned documents, and stories.

Searching Ancestry.com

You don't have to wait for Ancestry Hints to help you discover facts about your family, you can search the website any time you like.

Note: Although anyone can view Ancestry.com search results, you must have a subscription to view the actual records and images.

1. Click the **Web Search** button on the main toolbar.
2. Click "Ancestry.com" in the Search Locations list. If you want to research someone other than the individual who is currently selected, use the mini pedigree tree or Index of Individuals button to choose the appropriate person.

Notice that some fields have been filled in for you already.

By some fields you'll see an Exact Only checkbox. Use these options to limit your results to records that match your search terms exactly. Start by entering just one or two search terms, such as name and location.

3. Add or delete names, dates, and places as necessary.

4. To display records for a specific country or ethnicity first in your search results, choose an option from the **Collection Priority** drop-down list.

5. To limit your search results to a specific type of record:

    • Click the **Historical records** checkbox to search for birth records, censuses, military and immigration records, etc.

    • Click the **Stories & publications** checkbox to search for member-submitted stories, newspapers, and county histories.

    • Click the **Family trees** checkbox to search trees submitted by members.

    • Click the **Photos & maps** checkbox to search maps, historical images, and member-submitted photos.

6. Click **Search**.

7. If you get a large number of search results or matches, click the **Edit Search** button to narrow your search. Try adding more dates, a gender, or a spouse's name. (You can also narrow your search by clicking a category link on the top of the window.) If you get too few results or no matches, delete one or more of your search terms to broaden your search.

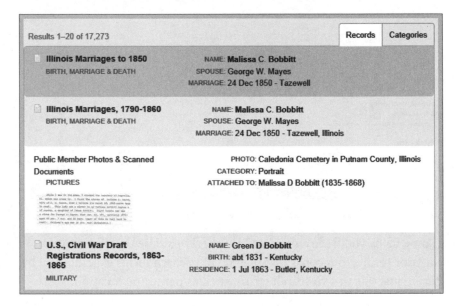

8. Click a search result to see the record or index. The tab at the bottom of the window lets you compare, side-by-side, the facts in your tree with the details found in the highlighted record.

9. If the information matches what you already know about the individual and his or her family, you can add the information to your tree. (For instructions see the next task.)

Search Tips

Ancestry automatically includes name variations, abbreviations, and nicknames when it searches for records. But if you're searching for an elusive ancestor, try these tips to get the most out of your searches:

- **Use wildcards.** Wildcards represent unknown letters in a name. Use an asterisk for up to six characters; a search for "fran*" will return results for Fran, Franny, Frank, Frannie, and Frankie; use a question mark for a single character; a search for "Hans?n" will return matches such as Hansen and Hanson.

- **Search for similar-sounding names.** You can search for last names that "sound like" the one you're looking for. For example, a search for Smith would return Smithe, Smyth, and Smythe. To use this type of search, click the "Restrict to exact" link under the individual's surname. Then click the **Soundex** and **Phonetic** checkboxes.

- **Estimate dates.** Not sure of the exact date of an event? Make an educated guess; you'll get better results than if you leave the field blank.

- **Add multiple locations.** If a family member lived in New York, Pennsylvania, and Illinois, add each of these residences to your search and you'll get results for all locations at once. To do this, click the "Show Advanced" link at the bottom of the search page. Then add additional locations in the event location fields.

- **Narrow your search by content.** Search for a specific type of content, such as family trees, historical records, or photo and maps. To do this, click the necessary checkboxes at the bottom of the search form.

- **Search in specific collections.** Ancestry has special collections focused on countries and ethnicities. If you're looking for an individual who lived in only one country, you can narrow your search to that location. Simply choose an option from the "Collection Priority" drop-down list.

Adding Ancestry.com Records to a Tree

When you find a relevant record or family tree on Ancestry.com, you can add the information directly to your tree using the Web Merge Wizard. You can choose the pieces of information you want to add and whether that information will be "preferred" or "alternate." The wizard can even include record images and sources for you automatically.

Note: It is always a good idea to save a backup of your file before making major changes using Web Merge.

1. In the Web Search workspace, access the Ancestry.com record or tree that you want to add to your tree.

2. Make sure the individual you want to add the record to is selected in the Person from Your Tree section. If you need to merge the record with a different person, click the **Select a Different Person** button (a file folder icon) in the toolbar. Choose an individual and click **OK**.

   The bottom of the window displays the information in your tree compared side-by-side with the information found in the Ancestry record.

3. Click **Merge**. The Web Merge Wizard will launch. Depending on the type of record you're accessing, the wizard may contain multiple pages.

   The left side of the window lists the names of the people included in the record you are adding. As you move through the wizard, each individual will be highlighted as you make decisions about his or her information.

Next to the individuals' names, you'll see two columns: the Person from My Tree column shows the information you already have in your tree and the Person from Web Search column shows the information from the record you are adding to your tree.

4. Use the buttons next to the facts in the two columns to determine how each fact will be added:

   • To keep a fact and mark it as "preferred," select the button next to the fact. The corresponding fact for the other individual will be added as an alternate fact unless you choose to discard it.

   • To remove a fact, click the arrow next to the Alternate heading and choose "Discard" from the drop-down list. This fact will not be added to your tree. Though you may choose to discard some facts for a person, it is usually a good idea to keep all facts in case they turn out to be relevant.

     If you discard a fact, you still have the option to add its source to your tree by clicking the **Keep sources** checkbox.

5. Click **Next** and do one of these options:

   • If the individual you want to add has parents, spouse(s), or children associated with the record, the wizard asks if you want to add the information found for the first additional family member. Continue with the next step.

- If the individual doesn't have siblings or parents associated with the record, click the **Next** button to go to the Summary window. Skip to step 8.

6. Choose what you want to do with each family member. You can ignore the person, add the person as a new individual in your tree, or merge the person with an existing individual in your tree.

   The details about the additional family members appear in the Person from Web Search column, while the information you already have in your tree appears in the Person from My Tree column. You can compare the information you have with what Family Tree Maker has found on Ancestry.com. If more than one individual appears in the Person from My Tree column, you will need to select the individual with whom you want to merge the new information.

7. Click **Next** and complete step 6 for every name in the record until all additional family members have been looked through. When you have made decisions for each family member, the Summary window opens.

8. Verify your selections in the Summary window. If you want to include an image of a record as a media item, click the **Media** checkbox. When you're ready, click **Merge Now**. A message tells you when the information has been successfully added to your tree. Click **OK** to close the message.

   Note: You *cannot* undo a merge. However, if you decide you made a mistake, you can simply delete the facts, people, and sources you added.

Searching Online with Family Tree Maker

With Family Tree Maker you have a convenient starting point for researching and expanding your family history—without interrupting your work. You can explore the Web using any of your favorite search engines or genealogy websites. Then use the Web-clipping tool to select text and images you're interested in and add them to individuals in your tree.

1. Click the **Web Search** button on the main toolbar. Using the mini pedigree tree or Index of Individuals button, choose the individual whose information you want to search for.

2. In Search Locations click the website that you want to search, or enter a website in the **Address** field of the Web browser. The website opens.

3. Look for information on your ancestors just as you would if you were performing any kind of online search.

Copying Online Facts

If you find details on a website that you'd like in your tree, you can use the Web-clipping tool. In some cases, Family Tree Maker will recognize the type of information you're viewing and will give you relevant fields to choose from. For example, if you add info from the Social Security Death Index, you'll have the option to add the text to a name, Social Security Number, birth fact, or death fact.

1. Access the website you want to copy facts from.

2. If you want to link the facts to a person in your tree who is different from the currently selected individual, click the **Select a different person** button in the Person from Your Tree section. Choose an individual and click **OK**.

3. Click the **Facts** tab at the bottom of the window. On the Search Result Detail toolbar, click the **Enable web clipping** button.

4. Move the mouse over text on the website until the pointer turns into a cursor. Highlight the text you want to copy. A drop-down list appears.

Name:	Pedersen, Mette K.	Occupation:	Gift
Age:	38	Destination:	NY.
Contract no.:	218200	Registration date:	10/5/1899
Birth place:	Tustrup, Aalbo		Fræer
Last res. parish:	Aalborg	Insert Fact ▾	Aalborg
		Name	
Last residence:	Aalborg		USA
Destination city:	New York City	Birth ▸	Date
Name of ship:	Indirekte	Marriage ▸	Place
IDcode:	I9899P3207	Death ▸	Description
		Other ▸	

5. Choose a fact from the **Insert Fact** drop-down list. For example, you can choose the birthplace fact. The highlighted information now appears in the Search Result Detail section.

Tip: You can copy multiple facts before adding the information to your tree; you don't need to add each fact individually.

6. When you have selected all the information you want, click **Merge**. The Web Merge Wizard will launch.

7. Use the buttons next to the facts in the two columns to determine how each fact will be added:

- To keep a fact and mark it as "preferred," select the button next to the fact. The corresponding fact for the other individual will be added as an alternate fact unless you discard it.

- To remove a fact, click the arrow next to the Alternate heading and choose "Discard" from the drop-down list. This fact will not be added to your tree. Though you may choose to discard some facts for a person, it is usually a good idea to keep all facts in case they turn out to be relevant.

If you discard a fact, you still have the option to add its source to your tree by clicking the **Keep sources** checkbox.

8. Click **Summary** to see how the information will be added to your tree. If necessary, click **Edit** to enter a source citation. (The default citation is the URL, or Web address, where the information was found.)

9. Click **Merge Now**. A message tells you when the information has been added successfully. Click **OK**.

Copying an Online Image

You may find family photos or historical documents that will enhance your family history. Family Tree Maker makes it easy to add these directly from a website to your tree.

Note: Before copying any images from the Web, make sure you aren't violating any copyrights and/or get permission from the owner.

1. Access the online image you want.

2. If you want to link the image to a person in your tree who is different from the currently selected individual, click the **Select a different person** button in the Person from Your Tree section. Choose an individual and click **OK**.

3. Click the **Media** tab at the bottom of the window. On the Search Result Detail toolbar, click the **Enable web clipping** button.

Search result detail ◀◀ Merge ⊘ 🖾 ✂

4. Move the mouse over the Web page until the image you want is highlighted by a green dotted line.

5. Click the highlighted image. A thumbnail of the image appears in the Search Result Detail section.

6. When you have selected all the images you want, click **Merge**. A message tells you when the image has been added successfully. Click **OK**.

    Note: The image will be linked to the person displayed in the Person from Your Tree section. You can also view it on the Media workspace.

Copying Online Text to a Note

While surfing the Web you may come upon interesting stories about the founding of your grandfather's hometown or a description of the ship your great-grandparents sailed to America on. You can easily save this type of information using the Web-clipping tool.

1. Access the website you want to copy text from.

2. If you want to link the notes to a person in your tree who is different from the currently selected individual, click the **Select a different person** button in the Person from Your Tree section. Choose an individual and click **OK**.

3. Click the **Notes** tab at the bottom of the window. To add the text as a personal note, click the **Person note** button; to add the text as a research note, click the **Research note** button.

4. On the Search Result Detail toolbar, click the **Enable web clipping** button.

5. Move the mouse over text on the website until the pointer turns into a cursor. Highlight the text you want to copy. The Insert note button appears.

6. Click **Insert note**. The information now appears in the Search Result Detail section.

7. Click **Merge**. A message tells you when the text has been added successfully. Click **OK**.

Note: The note will be linked to the person in the Person from Your Tree section. To view the notes later, go to the individual's Person tab and click the Notes tab at the bottom of the window.

Archiving a Web Page

Websites are constantly changing and even disappearing. If you find a website you want to refer to multiple times, or if you find a site that contains too much information to read in one sitting, you might want to archive the Web page. That way, you can read the page's contents and continue your research when it's convenient for you—without being connected to the Internet. When you archive a Web page, Family Tree Maker will save a "snapshot" of the page in HTML format that can be opened in any Web browser.

1. Access the Web page you want to archive.

2. If you want to link the archived page to a person in your tree who is different from the currently selected individual, click the **Select a different person** button in the Person from Your Tree section. Choose an individual and click **OK**.

3. Click the **Facts**, **Media**, or **Notes** tab. In the Search Result Detail toolbar, click the **Create page archive** button (a picture frame icon). A thumbnail of the page appears in the Search Result Detail section.

4. Click **Merge**. A message tells you when the archived Web page has been added successfully. Click **OK**.

Note: The archived page will be linked to the person in the Person from Your Tree section. To view the archived page later, go to the Media workspace.

Managing Research Websites

You can create a list of favorite family history websites so they're easy to visit.

Adding a Website to Your Favorites List

1. Click the **Web Search** button on the main toolbar. In Search Locations, click the **New** button.

2. If you are currently accessing the website, click the **Use Current Site** button. If not, enter the address for the website in the **URL address** field.

3. Enter a name for the website in the **Favorite name** field. This can be any name that helps you identify the website.

4. Click **OK**. The new website now appears in your list of personal favorites.

Sorting Your Website Favorites List

If you've gathered quite a few favorite sites, you can sort the list so it appears in an order that's useful to you. For example, if you visit some websites daily, you can put them at the top of the list.

1. Click the **Web Search** button on the main toolbar. Click **Manage Favorites**.

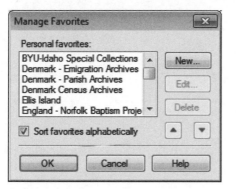

2. To display the websites in alphabetical order, click **Sort favorites alphabetically**. To choose your own display order for the websites, click a website in the Personal favorites list and then click the up and down arrows. When you're finished, click **OK**.

Part Three

Creating Charts, Reports, and Books

Chapter Nine
Creating Family Tree Charts

After spending time gathering, compiling, and entering your family's history, it's time to show off your hard work. Family Tree Maker offers a wide variety of family tree charts to help you bring your family history to life. Add your own personal touch by customizing the charts with attractive backgrounds, colors, photos, fonts, and more. These charts help you quickly view the relationships between family members and are also a fun way to share your discoveries—hang a framed family tree in your home, print out multiple copies to share at a family reunion, or email charts to distant relatives.

As you begin creating your own charts, you might want to experiment with various formatting options, print out different versions, and see what you like best.

Pedigree Charts

The pedigree chart is a standard tool of genealogists and what most people think of when they hear the term "family tree." This chart shows the direct ancestors of one individual—parents, grandparents, great-grandparents, and so on.

Standard Pedigree Charts

In the standard pedigree chart (fig. 9-1), the primary individual is on the left side of the tree, with ancestors branching off to the right—paternal ancestors on top and maternal ancestors on bottom.

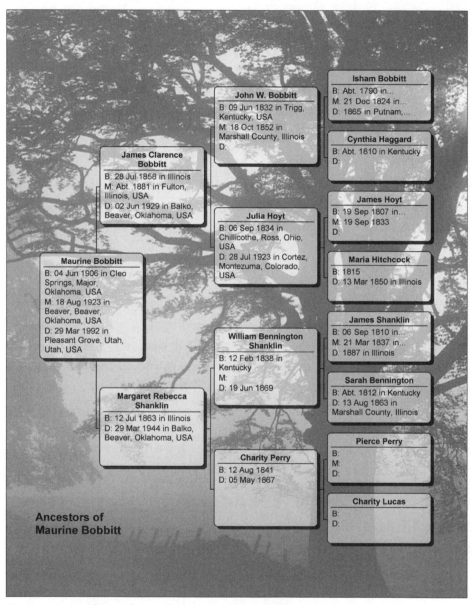

Figure 9-1. A pedigree chart using a custom template.

Vertical Pedigree Charts

In the vertical pedigree chart (fig. 9-2), the primary individual is shown at the bottom of the page, with his or her ancestors branching above the individual—paternal ancestors on the left and maternal ancestors on the right.

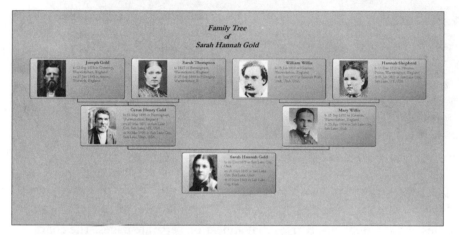

Figure 9-2. A customized vertical pedigree chart with portraits.

Hourglass Charts

An hourglass chart shows both the ancestors and descendants of an individual. The primary individual appears in the middle of the chart, with ancestors and descendants branching off in an hourglass shape.

Note: Because of its shape and the number of individuals included, most hourglass charts look best as posters.

Standard Hourglass Charts

In the standard hourglass chart, the primary individual appears in the middle of the chart, with ancestors branching above and descendants extending below the person.

The chart in figure 9-3 shows an hourglass chart laid out as a poster. Notice the white spaces running vertically and horizontally across the pages. These show the margins of a standard 8½" by 11" sheet of paper. If you want to print the tree at home, you can use these guides to tape the pages together.

Figure 9-3. An hourglass poster spread over six pages.

You can also create standard hourglass charts that are useful for including in family history books. When you use the book layout, the chart is condensed into a series of individual family trees that appear on separate pages. The chart in figure 9-4 shows one page of a multi-page book-layout chart. Notice the numbered box at the bottom right of the chart. When you are viewing the chart in Family Tree Maker, you can click one of these boxes to access that page of the chart. And when your chart is printed out, the numbered boxes help you navigate to related individuals found on other pages in the chart.

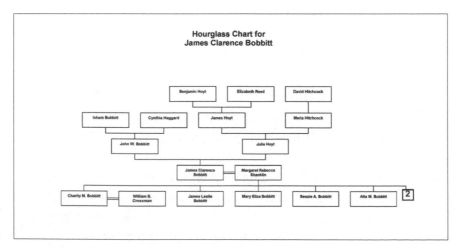

Figure 9-4. One page of a standard hourglass book chart.

Horizontal Hourglass Charts

In the horizontal hourglass chart (fig. 9-5), the primary individual appears in the middle of the chart with ancestors branching to the right and descendants extending to the left.

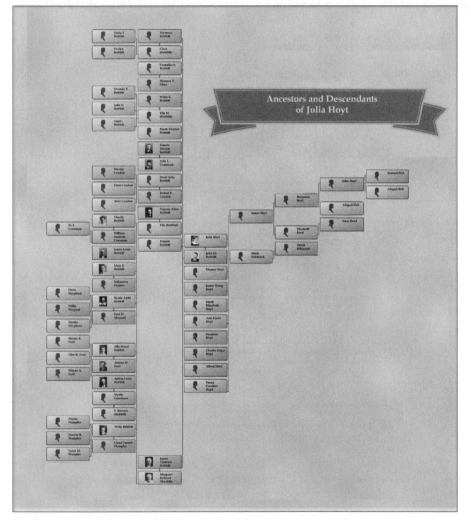

Figure 9-5. A horizontal hourglass chart with embellishments.

Descendant Charts

The descendant chart shows the direct descendants of an individual—children, grandchildren, great-grandchildren, and so on. The primary individual is shown at the top of the chart, with descendants underneath in horizontal rows. You can also create a chart that shows the direct line between two selected individuals (fig. 9-6).

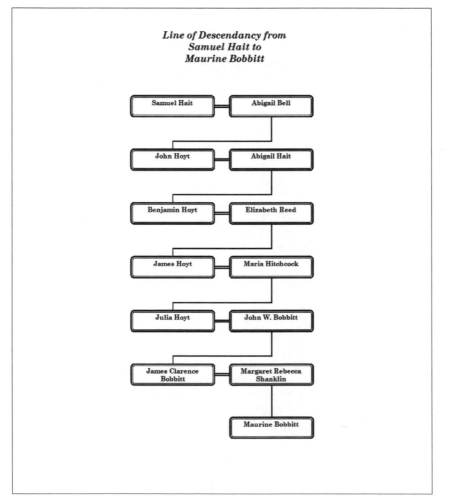

Figure 9-6. A direct-line descendant chart.

Bow Tie Charts

In the bow tie chart (fig. 9-7), the primary individual appears in the middle with paternal ancestors branching off to the left and maternal ancestors branching to the right.

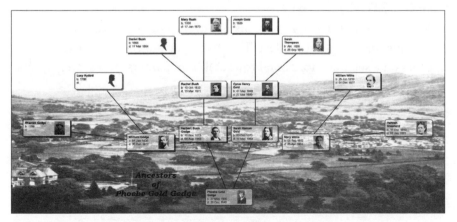

Figure 9-7. A customized bow tie chart.

Family Tree Charts

In the family tree chart (fig. 9-8), the primary individual appears at the bottom of the chart, with ancestors branching above him or her in a tree shape.

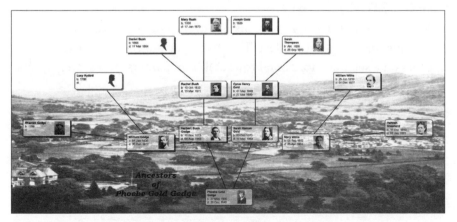

Figure 9-8. A customized family tree chart with images.

Fan Charts

A fan chart displays an individual's ancestors in a circular shape, one generation per level. The primary individual is at the center or bottom of the chart. You can choose between a full circle, semi-circle (fig. 9-9), quarter-circle, and more.

Note: Because of its shape and the number of individuals included, this chart is available only in poster layout.

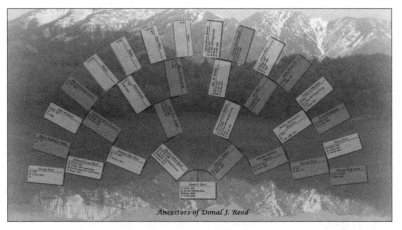

Figure 9-9. A customized semi-circle fan chart.

Extended Family Charts

The extended family chart (fig. 9-10) can display every individual you've entered in your tree or just the people you select. The chart is arranged so that each generation appears on a separate horizontal row: children, parents, and grandparents.

Note: Because of its shape and the number of individuals included, this chart is available only in poster layout.

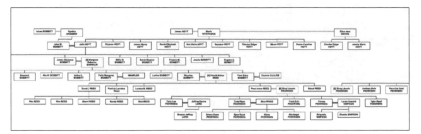

Figure 9-10. A section of a default extended family chart.

Relationship Charts

The relationship chart (fig. 9-11) is a graphical representation of one person's relationship to another. The common relative is shown at the top of the chart, with direct-line ancestors and descendants shown vertically beneath.

Figure 9-11. A relationship chart with a patterned background.

Creating a Chart

All charts are based on the last individual you were viewing in your tree. To change the primary individual in the chart, click his or her name in the mini pedigree tree above the chart, or click the Index of Individuals button and choose the person you want.

1. Go to the **Collection** tab on the Publish workspace. In Publication Types, click "Charts."

2. Double-click the chart icon, or select its icon then click the **Detail** tab.

3. Use the editing panel to change the chart.

Customizing a Chart

You can customize the contents and format of charts. For example, you can determine which facts are included and choose background images and fonts.

Note: You can save your custom changes as a template so you can use the same settings again. For instructions see "Creating Your Own Template."

Choosing Facts to Include in a Chart

In most charts you can choose which events or facts are included. Keep in mind, the more facts you add, the larger your chart will be.

1. Access the chart you want to change. In the editing toolbar, click the **Items to include** button.

The chart's default facts are shown in the Included facts list. You can add and delete facts and change their display options.

2. Do one of these options:

    *   To delete a fact, click the fact in the Included facts list and click the red (**X**) button.

- To add a fact, click the blue (+) button. The Select Fact window opens. Choose a fact from the list and click **OK**.

3. Change the fact options as necessary:

   - **Include only preferred facts.** Click this checkbox to include only preferred facts. If you have multiple facts for the same event, only the preferred is included.

   - **Include private facts.** Click this checkbox to include facts you've marked as private.

   - **Include blank facts.** Click this checkbox to include a fact label even if the fact is empty.

   - **Display user-defined short place name.** Click this checkbox to use shortened place names for locations.

4. To change a fact's format, click the fact in the Included facts list and click the **Options** button. Select the options you want and click **OK**.

   Note: Options vary by fact. For example, you can include dates and locations in births, marriages, and deaths.

5. Click the **Print individual number with name** checkbox to assign numbers to individuals in the chart.

6. Click **OK**.

Changing a Chart's Title

You can edit the title that appears at the top of a chart. Access the chart you want to change. In the editing panel, enter a name for the chart in the **Chart title** field.

Chart title: Ancestors of Julia Hoyt

Including Source Information with a Chart

While you can't display sources in the actual chart, you can add a list of sources to the end of a chart (fig. 9-12).

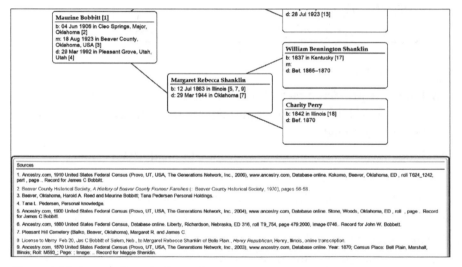

Figure 9-12. Sources for a pedigree chart.

1. Access the chart you want to change. In the editing toolbar click the **Items to include** button.

2. Click the **Include sources** checkbox; then click **OK**.

Adding Images and Text to a Chart

You can personalize your charts and make them more appealing by adding backgrounds, family photographs and portraits, or stories.

Adding a Background Image

Family Tree Maker comes with several attractive images you can use as chart backgrounds. Or you can create a background using images on your computer or photos in your tree.

1. Access the chart you want to change. In the editing panel choose an image from the **Background** drop-down list:

    *   To use an image on your computer, click **Browse for Image**. Choose an image and click **Open**.

    *   To use an image in your tree, click **Select from Media Collection**. Choose an image and click **OK**.

2. Choose how the background will be displayed. To center the image on the page, choose **Center**; to stretch the image to fit the entire page, choose **Stretch;** to show a close-up of the image, choose **Zoom**; to show a series of the image, choose **Tile**.

3. In the **Transparent** drop-down list, choose the intensity of the image. At 0 percent, the image will look normal, while a higher percentage will fade the image so the chart is easier to read.

Adding Portraits to a Chart

You can include images of individuals in a chart. In order to do this, you must have already added the images to your tree and linked them to specific individuals. (For instructions see "Adding a Portrait for an Individual" on page 81.)

1. Access the chart you want to change. Choose an image type from the
   Pictures drop-down list:

   - Choose **Thumbnail** to use low-resolution thumbnail images.

   - Choose **Photo** to use the resolution of the actual assigned photo.

2. From the top drop-down list, choose how images are positioned next to
   fact boxes:

   - To align images with the middle of boxes, choose **Center**.

   - To align images with the top of boxes, choose **Top**.

   - To resize images to the same height as boxes, choose **Stretch**.

     Note: This option may cause your photos to look distorted.

   - To resize images to the same height as boxes (with cropped margins
     on the left and right side), choose **Zoom**.

3. From the bottom drop-down list, choose how images are displayed in fact
   boxes:

   - To display images on the left side, choose **Left**.

   - To display images on the right side, choose **Right**.

   - To display images as a background, choose **Behind**.

4. If you want to change the size of the photo or thumbnail, enter a size in
   the **Inches wide** field.

   Note: The larger the image is, the less space available for facts.

5. Click **Use silhouettes** to display a silhouette for individuals who don't
   have portraits.

Adding a Decorative Photo or Embellishments

You can add family photographs, borders, or embellishments to your charts.

1. Access the chart you want to change. In the editing toolbar click the **Insert Image or Text Box** button.

2. Choose an image using the drop-down list:

   • To use an image on your computer, click **Insert from File**. Choose an image and click **Open**.

   • To use an image in your tree, click **Insert from Media Collection**. Choose an image and click **OK**.

   Note: You'll find a variety of decorative images in the Embellishments folder located in the Family Tree Maker folder.

3. To resize an image, click it. Then move the cursor over the icon in the bottom-right corner. Drag the image to the size you want.

4. To change the position of the image, move the mouse over the image and click and drag the image to the location you want.

Adding Text

You can add text anywhere on a chart. For example, you could write a short biography of the main person in the chart (fig. 9-13).

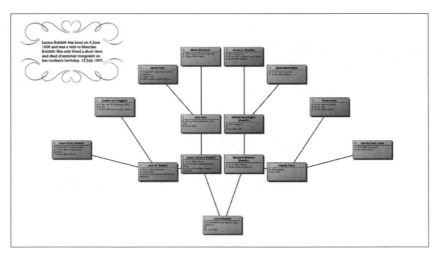

Figure 9-13. A family tree chart with a short biography.

1. Access the chart you want to add text to. In the editing toolbar click the **Insert Image or Text Box** button.

2. Choose "Insert Text Box" from the drop-down list.

3. To change the position of the text box, move the mouse over the text. When the cursor changes shape, click and drag the box to the location you want.

4. To enter or edit text, simply double-click the box. Enter your text and click **OK**.

    Tip: To change the text's size or color, click the **Fonts** button in the charts toolbar. In "Items to format" select "Text Boxes."

Changing the Header or Footer

You can define the headers and footers for each chart (the lines of text at the top and bottom of a chart).

1. Access the chart you want to change. In the editing toolbar click the **Header/Footer** button.

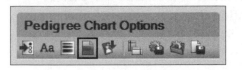

2. Change the header and footer options as necessary:

- **Chart note.** Enter any text you want to appear in the footer.
- **Draw box around footer.** Click this checkbox to enclose the footer in a box.
- **Print "Created with Family Tree Maker".** Click this checkbox to add this statement to the footer.
- **Include submitter info.** Click this checkbox to add your user information to the footer.
- **Include date of printing.** Click this checkbox to include the current date in the footer.

- **Include time of printing.** Click this checkbox to include the current time in the footer.

- **Include page/chart numbers.** Click this checkbox to include page numbers. From the drop-down list, choose whether the number appears in the header or the footer.

   In **Starting number** enter the number of the chart's first page; in **Starting number for continuation charts**, enter the number of the second page of the chart.

3. Click **OK**.

Changing Formatting for a Chart

You can change a chart's formatting such as its fonts, colors and borders, and box sizes.

Changing Layout Options

Depending on the number of individuals and facts in your chart, you may need to adjust the layout and spacing to best display each individual.

Note: Not every option is available in every chart.

1. Access the chart you want to change. The editing panel displays the options you can change.

2. Change the chart's layout options as necessary:

- **Layout.** Choose **Book** to create pages for a book; if a chart flows onto multiple pages, each page is cross-referenced to generations on other pages. Choose **Poster** to create pages that can be linked together to form a poster (click the **Advanced** button to customize the poster).

- **Overlap.** Change the horizontal spacing. Choose **No Overlap** to space columns equally; choose **Columns Overlap** to overlap columns slightly; choose **Only Root Overlaps** to overlap the primary individual's column with the parents' column; choose **Fishtail** to overlap all columns except for the last generation.

- **Spacing.** Change the vertical spacing. Choose **Perfect** to space rows evenly; choose **Collapsed** to space rows closer together; choose **Squished** to use minimal space between rows; choose **Custom** to adjust the spacing using the Advanced poster format.

  Tip: Collapse or squish columns if you want to fit many people on one page.

- **Align nodes.** Choose how lines connect individuals. Choose **Top** to use lines underneath names; choose **Center** to center lines next to each person; choose **Bezier** to use curved lines; choose **Straight** to use diagonal lines.

- **Center tree on page.** Click this checkbox to display the tree in the center of the page. If the chart is for a book, don't use this option. Instead, leave extra space in the left margin for binding.

- **Display last descendant generation vertically.** Click this checkbox to show the last generation under their parents.

- **Boxes overlap page breaks.** Click this checkbox so boxes that fall on a page break will not be split over two pages.

Adding Page Borders, Text Boxes, and Background Colors

You can enhance a chart by adding a border, background color, and text boxes.

1. Access the chart you want to change. In the editing toolbar click the **Box and line styles** button.

2. To change the format of text boxes, click a group in the Boxes list.

3. Change these options as necessary:

   • Choose border, fill, and shadow colors from the drop-down lists.

   • Click **Double line** to add two lines to box borders.

   • Click **Rounded corners** to use round corners for box borders.

   • Click **Semi-transparent** to make the background image or color partially visible through boxes.

   • Click **Use gradient fill** to make a box's fill color go from light to dark.

   • Click **All boxes same size** to make all boxes on the chart the same size.

4. To change the size of boxes, enter the maximum width and height (in inches) for boxes in the "Book layout maximums."

5. To change the format of pedigree and divider lines, choose colors from the drop-down lists. Then choose the line thickness.

6. To add a border to the entire chart, choose a color from the **Line** drop-down list. Then click **Double line** to add two lines to the page border; click **Rounded corners** to use round corners for the page border.

7. To add a colored background, choose the color from the Background drop-down list. (Choose "None" for a blank background.)

8. Click **OK**.

Changing Fonts

You can change the appearance of the text in charts to make it more formal, more fun, or maybe just more readable.

1. Access the chart you want to change. In the editing toolbar, click the **Fonts** button.

2. In the Items to format list, click the text element, such as the chart title, you want to change.

3. Choose a font from the **Font** drop-down list. You can also change the size of the font, its style, color, and alignment.

4. Click **OK** to save your changes.

Using Chart Templates

Family Tree Maker comes with several templates you can use to quickly dress up your family tree charts. You can also turn your own chart designs into templates.

Creating Your Own Template

After you've customized a chart with your favorite fonts and colors and changed the spacing and layout to make everyone fit perfectly on the page, you don't want to lose your settings. You can save your modifications as a template, and you won't have to recreate your changes if you want to use them on another chart.

1. After you have modified the chart, click the **Save settings** button in the editing toolbar.

2. Choose one of these options:

   • **Save as preferred template.** This option saves the current settings as the preferred template for all charts. However, this template isn't permanent; if you modify the preferred template, the old settings will be written over.

   • **Create new template.** This option lets you name the template and save it as a custom chart template.

3. Click **OK**. To assign your template to a chart see the next task.

Using a Custom Template

Family Tree Maker lets you use attractive templates to instantly change the look of your chart. You can apply custom templates to any chart. And if the results aren't exactly what you want, you can modify it.

1. Access the chart you want to apply a template to. Click the **Use saved settings** button in the editing toolbar.

2. Choose one of these template options:

    - **Default.** This is the default chart template.

    - **Preferred.** This is a template you have created and saved as your preferred template.

    - **Custom.** These are the custom templates found in Family Tree Maker (or templates you have created and saved).

3. Click **OK**.

Saving Charts

You can save a specific chart in Family Tree Maker, or you can save a chart in different file formats to export.

Saving a Specific Chart

If you like a chart you've created, you'll probably want to save it. That way you can view it again without having to recreate it.

1. After you've modified a chart, click the **Save chart** button in the editing toolbar.

2. Enter a unique name for the chart. For example, don't use generic terms like "Pedigree Chart" or "Relationship Chart."

3. Click **Save**.

    Tip: To open a saved chart, go to the Collection tab on the Publish workspace. In Publication Types, click **Saved Charts**. Then double-click the chart you want to open.

Saving a Chart as a File

You may want to save a chart as an image or PDF so you can share it easily with family or post it online.

1. Access the chart you want to save.

2. Click the **Share** button above the editing panel. From the drop-down list, choose one of these options:

    - **Export to PDF.** An Adobe PDF (Portable Document Format) is useful because it keeps the formatting you select. If you print a chart or send it to a relative, the chart will look exactly as you see it on your monitor. You can't change a PDF within Family Tree Maker, and you need Adobe Reader to view it. (Adobe Reader can be downloaded for free from the Adobe website.)

    - **Export to One Page PDF.** This option exports the chart as one page (regardless of size). Use this option if you're creating a poster-sized chart or printing a chart at a copy store.

    - **Export to Image.** This option lets you create an image of the chart as a bitmap, JPEG, or other image format.

    Each format has its own export options. After you choose a format type, you may be able to choose options such as page borders. Once you've made your selections, click **OK**.

3. Navigate to the location where you want to save the chart; then enter a name for the chart and click **Save**.

Printing a Chart

1. Access the chart you want to print.

2. Click the **Print** button above the editing panel.

3. When prompted choose a printer, select the number of copies, and choose a page range.

4. Click **Print**.

Sharing a Chart

You can share charts with others—via email—as a PDF.

Note: You must be connected to the Internet and have a desktop email program to use this feature.

1. Access the chart you want to email.

2. Click the **Share** button above the editing panel. From the drop-down list, choose **Send as PDF.**

3. Use the preview window to make sure the chart looks correct; then click **Send as PDF**.

4. Change any options as necessary and click **OK**.

5. Navigate to the location where you want to save the chart. Then enter a name for the chart and click **Save**. Family Tree Maker opens an email (with the file attached).

6. Send the email as you would any other.

Chapter Ten
Running Reports

Family Tree Maker includes a number of reports to help you organize and understand the information you've entered in your tree. You can create detailed reports about a single family, such as the family group sheet; relationship reports that show marriage events; bibliographies and source reports that help you keep track of your research; and more.

Each report can be customized—options differ by report. You can change fonts, add background images, and add headers and footers.

Genealogy Reports

Genealogy reports are a staple of serious family historians. These narrative reports contain biographical details about individuals. Relationships between people are shown using numbering systems that are unique to each report. You can choose from ancestor-ordered reports (Ahnentafels) or descendant-ordered reports.

Ahnentafel

The Ahnentafel (a German word meaning "ancestor table") is a numbered list of individuals (fig. 10-1). Its format is ancestor-ordered, meaning that it starts with one individual and moves backward in time to that individual's ancestors. This type of report isn't used frequently because it shows two family lines at the same time.

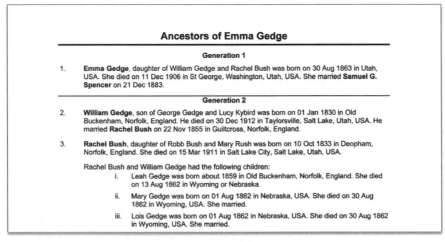

Figure 10-1. An Ahnentafel (ancestor report).

Descendant Report

A descendant report (fig. 10-2) is a narrative report that includes biographical information about each individual. It is descendant-ordered, meaning it starts with an individual and moves forward in time through that individual's children and grandchildren. You have four numbering system options: Register, NGSQ, Henry, and d'Aboville.

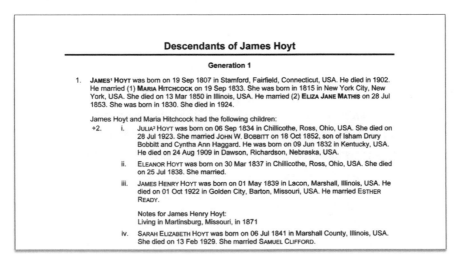

Figure 10-2. A Register descendant report.

Person Reports

Person reports give you an overview of your tree and help you focus on specific individuals.

Custom Report

Custom reports (fig. 10-3) let you explore your tree in ways that are interesting to you. For example, you can create a custom report of birthplaces or causes of death.

Residents of Illinois		
Albert Hoyt		
	Birth:	10 Feb 1848 in Marshall, Illinois
	Death:	10 Feb 1848 in Marshall, Illinois
Ann Hoyt		
	Birth:	20 Jul 1843 in Marshall, Illinois
	Death:	20 Jul 1843 in Marshall, Illinois
Charles Hoyt		
	Birth:	23 Sep 1846 in Marshall, Illinois
	Death:	Aug 1847
Charles Hoyt		
	Birth:	21 Oct 1857 in Marshall, Illinois
Cora Hewitt		
	Birth:	Abt. 1865 in Illinois
Cornelia Bobbitt		
	Birth:	Abt. 1856 in Illinois
Edwin Hewitt		
	Birth:	1832 in New York, USA
	Marriage:	Abt. 1853 in Pennsylvania or Illinois
Eugene Bobbitt		
	Birth:	Jan 1877 in Illinois
Francis Bobbitt		
	Birth:	Abt. 1869 in Illinois
Isham Bobbitt		
	Birth:	Abt. 1790 in Cerulean Springs, Trigg, Kentucky, USA
	Marriage:	21 Dec 1824 in Trigg, Kentucky
	Death:	1865 in Putnam, Illinois, USA
James Bobbitt		
	Birth:	28 Jul 1858 in Illinois
	Marriage:	Abt. 1881 in Fulton, Illinois, USA
	Death:	02 Jun 1929 in Balko, Beaver, Oklahoma, USA
	Burial:	02 Jun 1929 in Balko, Beaver, Oklahoma, USA
James Hoyt		
	Birth:	01 May 1839 in Marshall, Illinois
James Shanklin		
	Birth:	06 Sep 1810 in Fleming, Kentucky, USA
	Marriage:	1827 in Fulton, Illinois, USA
	Marriage:	21 Mar 1837 in Fulton, Illinois
	Marriage:	Bet. 1861–1870
	Death:	1887 in Illinois
Jennie Hoyt		
	Birth:	28 Jul 1861 in Marshall, Illinois
John Bobbitt		
	Birth:	09 Jun 1832 in Trigg, Kentucky, USA
	Marriage:	18 Oct 1852 in Marshall County, Illinois
	Burial:	14 Aug 1909 in Dawson, Nebraska, USA

Figure 10-3. A custom report showing all individuals who lived in Illinois.

Data Errors Report

The Data Errors Report (fig. 10-4) lists all instances where data is missing or may be incorrect. This includes nonsensical dates (e.g., an individual being born before his or her parents were born), empty fields, and duplicate individuals. (For more information see "Running the Data Errors Report" on page 251.)

Data Errors Report

Name	Birth Date	Potential Error
Anna Gedge	05 Sep 1865	The burial date occurred before his/her death.
Nathan Gedge	Abt. 1971	The birth date occurred after his/her mother was 60. The birth date occurred after his/her mother died. The birth date occurred after his/her father was 80. The birth date occurred more than one year after his/her father died.
Mette Katrina Pedersen		The individual has the same last name as her husband, Niels Pedersen.

Figure 10-4. A Data Errors Report.

Individual Report

The Individual Report (fig. 10-5) lists every fact and source you have recorded for a specific individual.

Individual Report for Cyrus Henry Gold

Individual Summary:	Cyrus Gold
Sex:	Male
Father:	Joseph Gold
Mother:	Sarah Thompson
Individual Facts:	
Name:	Cyrus Gold
Birth:	01 May 1848 in Birmingham, Warwick, England [1]
Death:	27 Mar 1930 in Salt Lake City, Salt Lake, Utah, USA [2]
Shared Facts:	**Mary Willis**
Marriage:	27 Mar 1871 in Salt Lake City, Salt Lake, Utah, USA [3]
Children:	Sarah Gold
	Cyrus Gold
	Thomas Gold
	Abraham Gold
	Alma Gold
	Lehi Gold

Figure 10-5. An Individual Report.

LDS Ordinances Report

The LDS Ordinances Report (fig. 10-6) is useful for members of The Church of Jesus Christ of Latter-day Saints and displays LDS-specific ordinances such as baptisms and sealings.

LDS Ordinances

Gedge, Herbert Bush
Birth:	10 Nov 1872 in Brighton, Salt Lake, Utah
Marriage:	20 Nov 1895 in Salt Lake City, Salt Lake, Utah
Death:	08 Sep 1942 in Salt Lake, Salt Lake City, Utah
Baptism (LDS):	10 Nov 1880
Endowment (LDS):	20 Nov 1895

Gedge, Phoebe Gold
Birth:	27 May 1900 in Salt Lake City, Salt Lake, Utah
Marriage:	15 Sep 1926 in Salt Lake City, Utah
Death:	28 Dec 1948 in Salt Lake City, Salt Lake, Utah
Endowment (LDS):	15 Sep 1926 in Salt Lake City, UT, USA

Gold, Sarah Hannah
Birth:	03 Dec 1873 in Salt Lake City, Utah
Marriage:	20 Nov 1895 in Salt Lake City, Salt Lake, Utah
Death:	05 Nov 1963 in Salt Lake City, Utah
Baptism (LDS):	03 Jan 1882

Figure 10-6. An LDS Ordinances Report.

List of Individuals Report

The List of Individuals Report has four options: all individuals in your tree, all individuals and their ID numbers, a list of anniversaries, a list of birthdays (fig. 10-7), and a contact list.

Birthday List

Name	Birth	Birthday	Death	Age
Gedge, William	01 Jan 1831	183	30 Dec 1912	81
Parsons, Elmer Wellington	04 Jan 1878	136	Dec 1960	82
Hansen, Mary Edna	07 Jan 1903	111	23 Jul 1945	42
Gedge, Wilford Gold	08 Jan 1909	105	04 Jul 1986	77
Gedge, Woodruff Gold	08 Jan 1909	105	05 Apr 1942	33
Pedersen, Jensine Pauline	10 Jan 1884	130	16 Jul 1964	80
Gedge, Herbert Gold	13 Jan 1902	112	05 Mar 1911	9
Walborn, Miranda	17 Jan 1847	167	21 Nov 1921	74
Lucas, Singleton Peak	18 Jan 1810	204	10 Mar 1877	67
Hewitt, Guy Edward	20 Jan 1884	130		
Wilcox, Nancy	25 Jan 1792	222	11 Dec 1866	74
Artz, Aaron	27 Jan 1853	161	18 Oct 1890	37
Bush, Sarah	28 Jan 1831	183		
Hewitt, Arthur Jay	29 Jan 1880	134		

Figure 10-7. A list of birthdays.

Notes Report

The Notes Report (fig. 10-8) lets you view the person, research, relationship, or fact notes you've entered in your tree.

Notes Report

Bobbitt, Lorine	**(04 Jun 1906 - 12 Jul 1907)**
Person Note:	Lorine died when she was 13 months old of what her twin Maurine called "summer complaint." Two other children died young, a boy and a girl.
Bush, Rachel	**(10 Oct 1833 - 15 Mar 1911)**
1900 U.S. Census Fact Not	() The 1900 census for Rachel Bush states that she is mother of ten children, 5 of whom are living.
Dawson, Nancy	**(? - 01 Dec 1857)**
Relationship Note:	(David Haggard) Sureties and witnesses are wedding are David Haggard, Martin Dawson, and Cary M. Carter.
Gedge, Flossie Gold	**(30 Oct 1904 - 09 Jul 1938)**
Person Note:	Married to Harrison Oliver. Probable burial in Blanding, Utah.
Gedge, Leah	**(Abt. 1859 - 13 Aug 1862)**
Person Note:	When Leah was barely three years old, her parents left England to travel to the United States. They joined the Homer Duncan Company in Nebraska and headed to Utah. She died enroute somewhere in Wyoming. Her death was followed by the death of her twin sisters who were born on the trail.

Figure 10-8. A report of person and relationship notes.

Surname Report

The Surname Report (fig. 10-9) lists the total number of individuals with a specific surname, the number of males and females with that surname, and the earliest and most recent year a surname appears in your tree.

Surname Report

Surname	Count	Male	Female	Earliest	Most recent
Hoyt	34	18	16	1740	1861
Gold	31	16	15	1825	1908
Bobbitt	27	12	15	1793	1909
Haggard	25	14	11	1678	1813
Gedge	23	11	12	1830	1914
Reed	15	7	8	1774	1901
Pedersen	12	7	4	1821	1973
Peterson	10	6	4	1888	1905
Shanklin	7	3	4	1810	1866
Thompson	7	4	3	1796	1835

Figure 10-9. A Surname Report sorted by name count.

Task List

A task list (fig. 10-10) displays all research tasks into your to-do list. You can see each task's priority, category, and creation and due dates.

Task List

☐	Write to Berks County Historical Society for Reed/Rieth church records	Priority: High Owner: General Task Categories: Reed Date Created: 3/24/2010 Date Due: 3/26/2010
☐	Write to Peoria County for Milton Hewitt's death record.	Priority: High Owner: General Task Categories: Hewitt Date Created: 2/17/2010 Date Due: 4/30/2010
☐	Look for marriage record for Joseph Thompson and "Jane" between 1840 and 1845 in Warwickshire, England	Priority: Medium Owner: General Task Categories: Records Date Created: 3/24/2010 Date Due: 6/30/2010

Figure 10-10. A research to-do list.

Timeline

A timeline (fig. 10-11) lists an individual's life events with the date and location of the event and the person's age at the time. You can also include events for an individual's immediate family (such as birth, marriage, and death) and historical events.

Timeline Report for John W. Bobbitt

	Yr/Age	Event	Date/Place
	1832	Birth	09 Jun 1832 Kentucky, USA
	1834 2	Birth (Spouse) Julia Hoyt	06 Sep 1834 Chillicothe, Ross, Ohio, USA
	1850 17	1850 U.S. Census	1850 Tazewell County, Illinois, USA
	1852 20	Marriage Julia Hoyt	18 Oct 1852
	1854 21	Birth (Son) Seymour Bobbitt	Abt. 1854 Illinois, USA
	1857 24	Birth (Daughter) Cornelia O. Bobbitt	Mar 1857 Illinois, USA
	1858 26	Birth (Son) James Clarence Bobbitt	28 Jul 1858 Illinois, USA

Figure 10-11. A timeline for an individual and his family.

Relationship Reports

Relationship reports are just what they sound like; they show the relationships between different individuals and families in your tree.

Family Group Sheet

A family group sheet (fig. 10-12) is one of the most commonly used reports in family history. It is a detailed report about a single family (primarily the parents and children of a family, although it also includes the names of the couple's parents); including names, birth, death, and marriage information; notes; and sources. If the individual has more than one spouse, additional family group sheets will be created for each family.

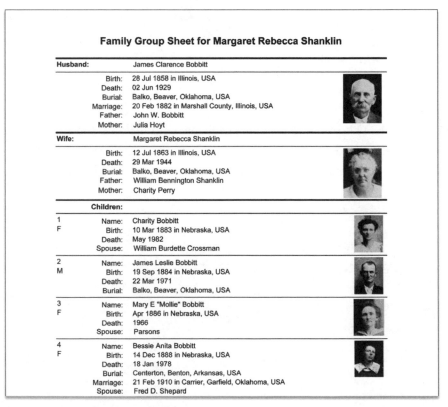

Figure 10-12. A family group sheet.

Family View Report

The Family View Report (fig. 10-13) shows three generations of ancestors for an individual and his or her parents and children.

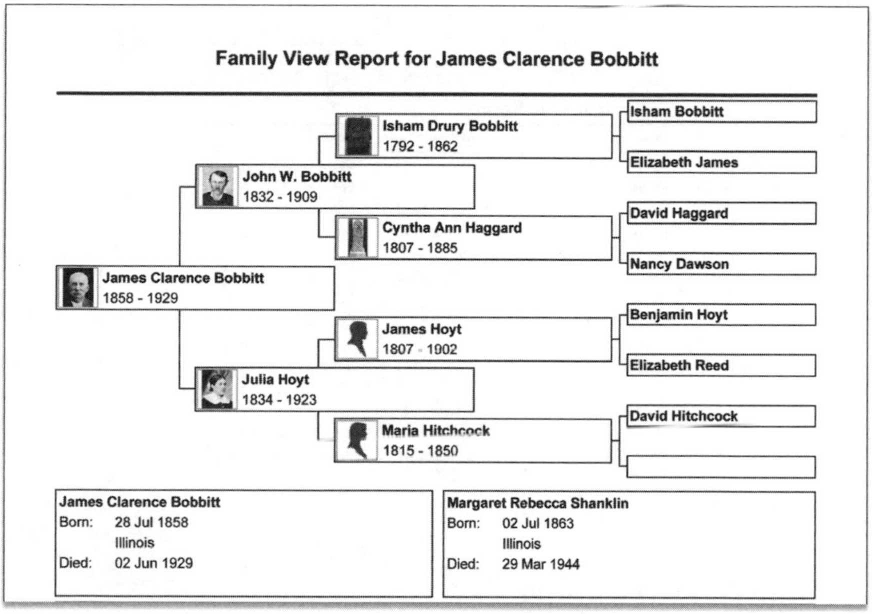

Family View Report for James Clarence Bobbitt

Figure 10-13. A Family View Report.

Kinship Report

The Kinship Report (fig. 10-14) helps you determine how individuals in your tree are related to a specific person.

Kinship Report for Maria Hitchcock

Name:	Birth Date:	Relationship:	Civil:	Canon:
(Hoyt), John Hait	24 Nov 1740	Father of father-in-law		
Bobbitt, Alta M.	09 Feb 1892	Great granddaughter	III	3
Bobbitt, Arthur L.	24 Aug 1897	Great grandson	III	3
Bobbitt, Bessie A.	14 Dec 1888	Great granddaughter	III	3
Bobbitt, Charity M.	10 Mar 1883	Great granddaughter	III	3
Bobbitt, Cornelia	Abt. 1856	Granddaughter	II	2
Bobbitt, Eugene A.	Jan 1877	Grandson	II	2
Bobbitt, Fern Edna	25 Feb 1909	Great granddaughter	III	3

Figure 10-14. A Kinship Report.

Marriage Report

The Marriage Report (fig. 10-15) shows a husband and wife, their marriage date, and relationship status. Unlike other reports, you cannot choose which individuals are included.

Marriage Report

Husband:	Wife:	Marriage Date:	Relation:
Andersen, Peder Christian	Nielsdatter, Maren		Spouse - Ongoing
Andersen, Peder Christian	Peterson, M. K.		Spouse - Ongoing
Bennington, William Jr.	Smith, Margaret	16 Apr 1793	Spouse - Ongoing
Bobbitt, Isham Drury	Haggard, Cyntha Ann	21 Dec 1824	Spouse - Ongoing
Bobbitt, James Clarence	Shanklin, Margaret Rebecca	20 Feb 1882	Spouse - Ongoing
Bobbitt, John W.	Hoyt, Julia	18 Oct 1852	Spouse - Ongoing
Bush, Robb	Rush, Mary		Spouse - Ongoing
Dawson, Martin	Carter, Elizabeth		Spouse - Ongoing
Gedge, George	Kybird, Lucy		Spouse - Ongoing
Gedge, Herbert Bush	Gold, Sarah Hannah	20 Nov 1895	Spouse - Ongoing
Gedge, Reames	Kybird, Lucy		Spouse - Ongoing
Gedge, William	Bush, Rachel	22 Nov 1855	Spouse - Ongoing
Gold, Cyrus Henry	Newman, Louisa Fanny	08 Aug 1904	Spouse - Ongoing
Gold, Cyrus Henry	Willis, Mary	27 Mar 1871	Spouse - Ongoing

Figure 10-15. A Marriage Report.

Outline Descendant Report

The Outline Descendant Report (fig. 10-16) starts with an ancestor and outlines each generation of descendants; you can choose the number of generations to show in the report.

Outline Descendant Report for Abigail Hait

..... 1   Abigail Hait b: 09 Oct 1740 in Stamford, Fairfield, Connecticut, USA, d: 27 Feb 1796 in Stamford, Fairfield, Connecticut, USA
.....   + John Hoyt b: 24 Nov 1740 in Stamford, Fairfield, Connecticut, USA, m: 31 Dec 1761, d: 01 Mar 1825
....   2   Samuel Hoyt b: 08 Nov 1762 in Stamford, Fairfield, Connecticut, USA, d: 22 Sep 1838 in Stamford, Fairfield, Connecticut, USA
....   2   William Hoyt b: 01 Aug 1764 in Stamford, Fairfield, Connecticut, USA, d: 25 Aug 1828
....   2   John Hoyt b: 02 Dec 1765 in Stamford, Fairfield, Connecticut, USA, d: 15 Dec 1812 in Burlington, Chittenden, Vermont, USA
....   2   Abigail Hoyt b: 31 Oct 1767 in Stamford, Fairfield, Connecticut, USA, d: 26 Aug 1840 in Norwalk, Fairfield, Connecticut, USA
....   2   Benjamin Hoyt b: 19 Feb 1769 in Stamford, Fairfield, Connecticut, USA, d: 21 Nov 1813
....   + Elizabeth Reed b: 15 Nov 1774, m: 23 Dec 1792, d: 11 Jun 1818
....   3   Sarah Hoyt b: 23 Feb 1794 in Tarrytown, Westchester, New York, USA
....   3   Seymour Hoyt b: 22 Mar 1796 in Stamford, Fairfield, Connecticut, USA, d: 29 Oct 1866 in Stamford, Fairfield, Connecticut, USA
....   3   Benjamin Hoyt b: 28 Jul 1798 in Stamford, Fairfield, Connecticut, USA, d: 13 Feb 1801 in

Figure 10-16. An Outline Descendant Report.

Parentage Report

The Parentage Report (fig. 10-17) lists each individual, his or her parents, and their relationship (e.g., biological, adopted, foster).

Parentage Report

Name	Parents	Relationship
Andersen, Peder Christian		
Bell, Permelia		
Benfell, Edith Annie		
Bennington, Constance	Bennington, William Jr.	Biological
	Smith, Margaret	Biological
Bennington, Mary Elizabeth	Bennington, William Jr.	Biological
	Smith, Margaret	Biological
Bennington, Sarah	Bennington, William Jr.	Biological
	Smith, Margaret	Biological

Figure 10-17. A Parentage Report.

Place Usage Report

The Place Usage Report (fig. 10-18) lists the locations in your tree and each person associated with it. You can also include specific events, such as birth or marriage, that occurred at that location.

Place Usage Report

Albemarle County, Virginia, USA
Haggard, David
   Birth: 1763
Haggard, Nathaniel
   Birth: 21 Nov 1723

Ålborg, Nordjylland, Denmark
Pedersen, Mette
   Res: May 1924
Pedersen, Mette Katrina
   Emigr: 05 Oct 1899
Pedersen, Niels
   Emigr: 20 Apr 1899
Pedersen, Oliver Cowdery
   Birth: 26 Apr 1891
   Emigr: 05 Oct 1899

Aston Manor, Warwick, England
Gold, Joseph
   Occu: 1861 Bricklayer

Aston, Warwick, England
Gold, Joseph
   Marr: 27 Jan 1845
   Marr: 30 Jun 1861
   Marr: 20 Jun 1861

Figure 10-18. A Place Usage Report.

Media Reports

Media reports let you view items individually or in groups.

Media Item Report

A Media Item Report (fig. 10-19) shows an image (or icon) of a media item, its caption, date of origin, description, and individuals linked to the item.

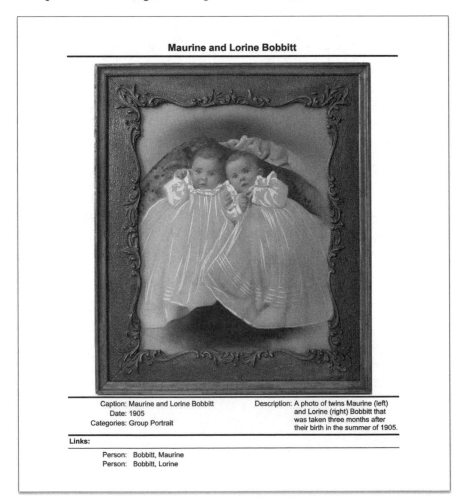

Figure 10-19. A Media Item Report.

Media Usage Report

The Media Usage Report (fig. 10-20) lists all your media items. For each item you'll see a thumbnail, name, location on your computer, and sources it is linked to.

Media Usage Report

Records of the olden time, or, Fifty years on the prairies : embracing sketches of the discovery, exploration and settlement of
> File Location: C:\Documents and Settings\tlord\Desktop\Family Tree Maker\ReedPedersen_2009 Media\records.tmp
>
> Source Ancestry.com, Records of the olden time, or, Fifty years on the prairies :
> Citation: embracing sketches of the discovery, exploration and settlement of (Provo, UT, The Generations Network, Inc., 2005), www.ancestry.com, Database online. Record for.
>
> Source Ancestry.com, Records of the olden time, or, Fifty years on the prairies :
> Citation: embracing sketches of the discovery, exploration and settlement of (Provo, UT, The Generations Network, Inc., 2005), www.ancestry.com, Page 768.

Reed 1930 Census
> File Location: C:\Documents and Settings\tlord\Desktop\Family Tree Maker\ReedPedersen_2009 Media\Media0010.jpg
>
> Source 1930 United States Federal Census, www.ancestry.com.
> Citation:

Reed California Home c. 1930
> File Location: C:\Documents and Settings\tlord\Desktop\Family Tree Maker\ReedPedersen_2009 Media\Media0149.jpg

Figure 10-20. A Media Usage Report.

Photo Album

A photo album (fig. 10-21) shows a person's birth and death dates, the names of their parents, and all photos linked to them.

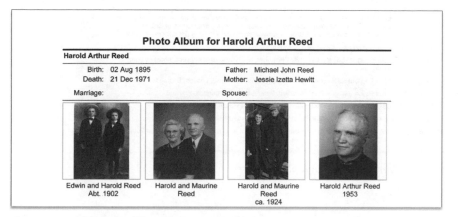

Figure 10-21. A photo album for an individual.

Source Reports

Family Tree Maker includes several reports that help you see how you've sourced facts in your tree.

Bibliography

A bibliography (fig. 10-22) is a detailed list of all the sources used in your research.

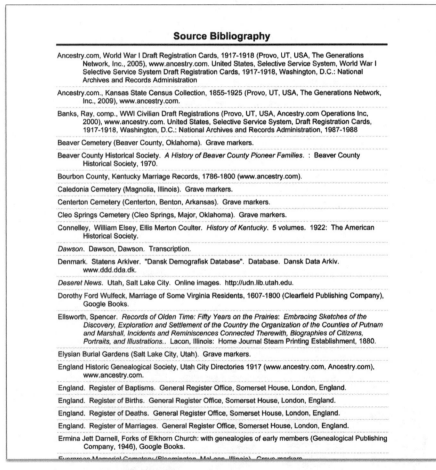

Figure 10-22. An annotated bibliography.

Documented Facts Report

The Documented Facts Report (fig. 10-23) shows an individual and the events you've entered source information for.

Figure 10-23. A Documented Facts Report.

Undocumented Facts Report

The Undocumented Facts Report (fig. 10-24) shows individuals and events that don't have sources associated with them.

Figure 10-24. An Undocumented Facts Report.

Source Usage Report

The Source Usage Report (fig. 10-25) shows each source and the individuals and facts associated with it.

Source Usage Report

Source Title: **1850 United States Federal Census**
Repository: www.ancestry.com
Citation: Ancestry.com, 1850 United States Federal Census (Provo, UT, USA, The Generations Network, Inc., 2005), www.ancestry.com, Database online. Year: 1850; Census Place: District 1, Fleming, Kentucky; Roll: M432_199; Page: 346A; Image:. Record for Sarah Shanklin. [Source citation includes media item(s)]
Bennington, Sarah

Source Title: **1860 United States Federal Census**
Repository: www.ancestry.com
Citation: Ancestry.com, 1860 United States Federal Census (Provo, UT, USA, The Generations Network, Inc., 2004), www.ancestry.com, Database online. Year: 1860; Census Place: Bell Plain, Marshall, Illinois; Roll: ; Page: ; Image:. Record for Sarah Shanklin. [Source citation includes media item(s)]
Bennington, Sarah

Figure 10-25. An Source Usage Report.

Calendars

You can make calendars (fig. 10-26) that display birthdays, death dates, and anniversaries for your immediate family or ancestors.

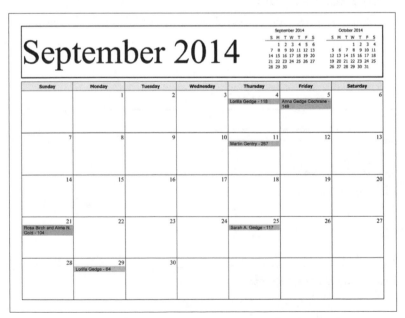

Figure 10-26. A calendar showing birth dates for all individuals.

Creating a Report

All reports are based on the last individual you were viewing in your tree. To change the primary individual in the report, click his or her name in the mini pedigree tree above the report, or click the Index of Individuals button and choose the person you want.

1. Go to the **Collection** tab on the Publish workspace. In **Publication Types**, click the report type you want.

2. Double-click the report icon, or select its icon and then click the **Detail** tab.

3. Use the editing panel to change the report.

Customizing a Report

You can customize the contents and format of reports. For example, you can determine which individuals and facts are included in the report and choose background images and fonts.

Choosing Facts to Include in a Report

In some reports you can choose which events or facts you'd like to include.

1. Access the report you want to change. In the editing toolbar click the **Items to include** button.

The Items to Include window opens. The report's default facts are shown in the Included facts list. You can add and delete facts and change their display options.

2. Do one of these options:

   • To delete a fact click the fact in the Included facts list and click the red (**X**) button.

   • To add a fact click the blue (+) button. The Select Fact window opens. Choose a fact from the list and click **OK**.

3. Change the fact options as necessary:

    • **Include only preferred facts.** Click this checkbox to include only preferred facts. If you have multiple facts for the same event, only the preferred is included.

    • **Include private facts.** Click this checkbox to include facts you've marked as private.

    • **Include blank facts.** Click this checkbox to include a fact label even if the fact is empty.

    • **Display user-defined short place name.** Click this checkbox to use shortened place names for locations.

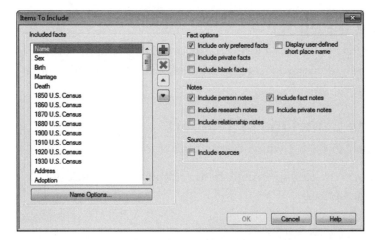

4. To change a fact's format, click the fact in the Included facts list and click the **Options** button. Select the options you want and click **OK**.

Note: Options vary by fact. For example, you can include dates and locations in births, marriages, and deaths.

5. Choose which notes to include in the report:

    • Click **Include person notes** to show person notes linked to individuals.

    • Click **Include research notes** to show research notes linked to individuals.

    • Click **Include relationship notes** to show person notes linked to relationships.

    • Click **Include fact notes** to show notes linked to facts.

    • Click **Include private notes** to show a note even if it has been marked as private.

6. To show sources in the report, click the **Include sources** checkbox.

7. Click **OK**.

Choosing Individuals to Include in a Report

In many reports you can choose which individuals will be included. For example, you can choose a specific ancestor and his or her descendants. You can also choose individuals by picking specific criteria (for example, you may want to generate a report that shows all individuals who were born in a particular city).

1. Access the report you want to change. You can choose individuals for the report in the editing panel.

2. Do one of these options:

   - To include the individual's immediate family members, click **Immediate family**.

   - To include everyone in your tree, click **All individuals**.

   - To choose specific individuals, click **Selected individuals**. The Filter Individuals window opens. Click a name and then click **Include** to add the person. When you're finished choosing individuals click **OK**.

Changing a Report's Title

You can change the title that appears at the top of a report. Access the report you want to change. In the editing panel, enter a new name in the **Report title** field.

Adding a Background Image

Family Tree Maker comes with several attractive images you can use as report backgrounds. Or you can create a background using images on your computer or photos in your tree.

1. Access the report you want to change. In the editing panel choose an image from the **Background** drop-down list:

   - To use an image on your computer, click **Browse for Image**. Choose an image and click **Open**.

   - To use an image in your tree, click **Select from Media Collection**. Choose an image and click **OK**.

   ```
   Background:   Tree_2                  ▼

                 80  % transparent  ▲▼  Tile    ▼
   ```

2. Choose how the background will be displayed. To center the image on the page, choose **Center**; to stretch the image to fit the entire page, choose **Stretch**; to show a close-up of the image, choose **Zoom**; to show a series of the image, choose **Tile**.

3. In the **Transparent** drop-down list, choose the intensity of the image. At 0 percent, the image will look normal, while a higher percentage will fade the image so the report is easier to read.

Changing the Header or Footer

You can define a report's headers and footers (the lines of text at the top and bottom of the page).

1. Access the report you want to change. In the editing toolbar click the **Header/Footer** button.

2. Change the header and footer options as necessary:

- **Show report title on every page.** Click this checkbox to display a header (the title) on each page of the report.

- **Show footer.** Click this checkbox to display a footer on each page of the report. Click **Include page number** to display a page number on the left side of the footer; click **Include print date** to display the current date on the right side of the footer; click **Include print time** to display the current time next to the current date.

3. Click **OK**.

Changing Fonts

You can change the appearance of the text in reports to make it more formal, more fun, or maybe just more readable.

1. Access the report you want to change. In the editing toolbar click the **Fonts** button.

2. In the Items to format list, click the text element, such as the report title, you want to change.

3. Choose a font from the **Font** drop-down list. You can also change the size of the font, its style, color, and alignment.

4. Click **OK** to save your changes.

Saving Reports

You can save a specific report in Family Tree Maker, or you can save a report in different file formats to export.

Saving the Settings for a Report

After you've customized a report, you can save your settings so you won't have to recreate these changes the next time you view the report. The settings you can save depend on the report, but generally include fact options, fonts, headers and footers, page layouts, and background images.

Note: You cannot save settings in one report and use them in another. For example, if you save settings in the Parentage Report, you cannot use these settings in the Kinship Report.

1. After you've modified the report, click the **Save settings** button in the editing toolbar.

2. A message asks if you want to use the current settings as the preferred settings for this report type. Click **Yes**.

    Tip: To change back to the report's default settings, click the **Use report settings** button in the editing toolbar. Then choose **Default settings** and click **OK**.

Saving a Specific Report

If you like a report you've created, you'll probably want to save it. That way you can view it again without having to recreate it.

1. After you've modified a report, click the **Save report** button in the editing toolbar.

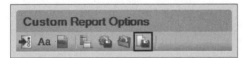

2. Enter a unique name for the report. For example don't use generic terms like "Family Group Sheet" or "Custom Report."

3. Click **Save**.

    Tip: To open a saved report, go to the Collection tab on the Publish workspace. In Publication Types click **Saved Reports**. Then double-click the report you want to open.

Saving a Report as a File

You may want to save a report as a document or spreadsheet so you can share it easily with family or post it online.

1. Access the report you want to save.

2. Click the **Share** button above the editing panel. From the drop-down list, choose one of these options:

   - **Export to PDF.** An Adobe PDF (Portable Document Format) is useful because it keeps the formatting you select. If you print a report or send it to a relative, the report will look exactly as you see it on your monitor. You can't change a PDF within Family Tree Maker, and you need the Adobe Reader to view it. (Reader can be downloaded for free from the Adobe website.)

   - **Export to CSV.** This spreadsheet format organizes information into fields (comma-separated values). Although you can export any report to a CSV file, it is most useful for statistical reports that use columns, such as the marriage report.

   - **Export to RTF.** This creates a basic text file but can include information such as text style, size, and color. This universal format can be read by nearly all text editors.

   - **Export to HTML.** Hypertext Markup Language is the standard language for creating and formatting Web pages.

   Each format has its own export options. After you choose a format type, you may be able to choose options such as text separators. Once you've made your selections, click **OK**.

3. Navigate to the location where you want to save the report. Then enter a name for it and click **Save**.

Printing a Report

When you are done creating and customizing a report, you may want to print it. Family Tree Maker makes it easy to choose setup options and print a report.

1. Access the report you want to print.

2. Click the **Print** button above the editing panel.

3. When prompted choose a printer, select the number of copies, and choose a page range.

4. Click **Print**.

Sharing a Report

You can share reports with others—via email—in a variety of formats.

Note: You must be connected to the Internet and have a desktop email program to use this feature.

1. Access the report you want to email.

2. Click the **Share** button above the editing panel. From the drop-down list, choose one of these options:

    *   **Send as PDF.** The Adobe PDF retains printer formatting and graphical elements so it resembles how the printed document will appear.

    *   **Send as CSV.** This format organizes information into fields (comma-separated values) and is meant to be imported into spreadsheet programs.

    *   **Send as RTF.** This creates a basic text file but can include information such as text style, size, and color. This universal format can be read by nearly all text editors.

    *   **Send as Image.** This option lets you create an image of the report as a bitmap, JPEG, or other image format.

    Each format has its own export options. After you choose a format type, you may be able to choose options such as page borders and text separators. Once you've made your selections, click **OK**. A file management window opens.

3. Navigate to the location where you want to save the report. Then enter a name for the report and click **Save**. Family Tree Maker opens a new email (with the file attached).

4. Send the email as you would any other.

Chapter Eleven
Creating a Family History Book

Wouldn't you love to have a printed family history to share your family stories, photographs, maps, and research? And what could be more convenient than using the same software to organize your family history *and* create a book to tell your ancestral story?

Family Tree Maker has two publishing tools to help you create a quality family history book that you and your family will enjoy for years to come. The first is a desktop book-building feature built into the Family Tree Maker software. It's a great way to assemble a traditional genealogy using images, facts, charts, and reports from your tree. The second tool is MyCanvas, a Web-based publishing service. It's perfect for creating scrapbooks, photo books, and more informal family histories.

The Desktop Book-Building Tool

Getting started with the book-building tool is easy because you can use the facts, charts, reports, and timelines already in your tree. Add some personal stories and photos and you've created a book you can email to family members or get printed at a copy shop.

Starting a Family History Book

1. Go to the **Collection** tab on the Publish workspace. In **Publication Types**, click **Books**.

2. Double-click **Genealogy Book**. The Save Book window opens.

3. Enter a title for the book in the **Book name** field and click **Save**. The book opens in the text editor.

Importing a Book

If you created a book in Family Tree Maker 2006 or Version 16, you can import the book into your tree. However, because of differences between the old and new software, some items won't transfer, such as images, text formatting, and NGSQ reports.

Note: Before you import a book, make a backup of your tree. Also, you can only import books that have been created in Family Tree Maker.

1. Choose **File>Import Books**.

2. Navigate to the Family Tree Maker (.ftw) file that contains the book you want to import and click **Open**. A success message shows how many books and book items were imported.

3. Click **OK**. The book is added to the Saved Books list.

4. To view the imported book, go to the **Collection** tab on the Publish workspace. In **Publication Types**, click **Saved Books**.

5. Double-click the book to open it in the text editor.

    If an item wasn't imported, you can click on the missing item in the outline to see an explanation of what has been left out—and in some cases, who the item was attached to.

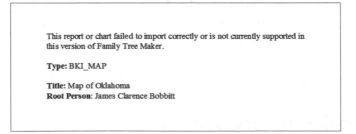

Accessing a Saved Book

1. Go to the **Collection** tab on the Publish workspace. In **Publication Types**, click **Saved Books**.

2. Double-click the book you want to open, or select its icon and then click the **Detail** tab. The book opens in the text editor.

Setting Up a Book

When you create a book you can enter the name of the author and title and add headers and footers.

1. Access the book you want to set up.

2. In the book panel toolbar, click the **Book Properties** button.

3. Change the book's properties as necessary:

   - **Book title.** Enter the name of the book. This is the title that will appear in the book's headers and footers; it is not entered on the title page automatically.

   - **Author.** Enter the author of the book.

   - **Header.** Choose a header type from the drop-down list. Headers are typically the title of a book, but you can have no header, or a combination of the book title, chapter name, and page number. To change the header's font, click **Font** and choose a style and size from the drop-down list.

     Note: You can change the header for a specific page using Item Properties. For instructions see "Changing an Item's Settings."

- **Footer.** Choose a footer type from the drop-down list. Footers are typically page numbers, but you can have no footer, or a combination of the book title, chapter name, and page number. To change the footer's font, click **Font** and choose a style and size from the drop-down list.

  Note: You can change the footer for a specific page using Item Properties. For instructions see "Changing an Item's Settings."

- **Starting number.** Choose what page you want the body of the book to start on (the front matter—title page, table of contents, dedication, etc.—will be numbered separately).

- **Use Roman numerals.** Click this checkbox to use standard Roman numerals (i, ii, iii, iv) for the book's front matter—title page, table of contents, dedication, etc.

4. Click **OK**.

Adding Content to a Book

You can add any number of items to your family history book, including stories, photos, reports, charts, and even an automatically generated table of contents and index.

Adding Text

Don't let your family history book become a dry recitation of facts. Add interest by including family stories and memories. If your grandfather immigrated to America when he was young, don't just list this fact in an individual report. Include a photo of the ship your grandfather arrived on and an excerpt from his journal that tells how he felt when he saw the Statue of Liberty.

Family Tree Maker has three options for entering text: you can manually type text, import text from a text file or document, or use Smart Stories to extract facts, sources, and notes in your tree (for more information on Smart Stories, see page 54).

Adding a Text Item

Before you can add stories, you'll need to add a text item to the book. A text item is basically a blank sheet of paper in the book text-editor. Creating one is much like opening a new document in a word-processing program. You can use it for everything from an entire chapter to a simple page with a photo and a caption.

1. Access the book you want to add a text item to. In the book panel toolbar, click the **Add Book Item** (+) button.

The Add Book Item window opens.

![Add Book Item window showing Publication type list on the left (Charts & Reports, Charts, Genealogy Reports, Person Reports, Relationship Reports, Place Reports, Media Reports, Source Reports, Other, Saved Publications, Saved Charts, Saved Reports, Saved Smart Stories (Media)) and item icons on the right: Calendar Report, Smart Story (Text Item), Table of Contents, Index, Place Holder]

2. In **Publication type**, click **Other**. Then double-click **Text Item**, or select its icon and then click **OK**. A blank page opens in the text editor.

Entering Text Manually

You can use the text editor to write your own family narratives.

1. Click a text item in the book outline.

2. Place the cursor where you want the text and begin typing.

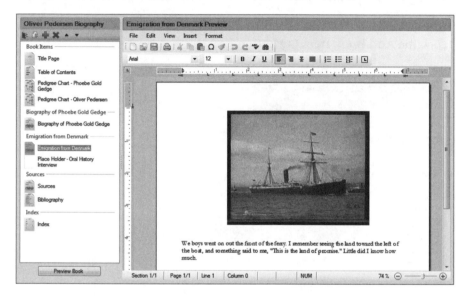

Importing Text from Another Document

If you've already written part of your book in another text editor, you don't have to re-type your text or copy and paste sections into Family Tree Maker. You can import the entire document at once—without losing formatting.

1. Click a text item in the book outline.

2. Place the cursor where you want the text. In the text editor choose **File>Open**. A file management window opens.

3. Navigate to the document you want to import and click **Open**.

Formatting Text

The text formatting options available in Family Tree Maker are similar to most word-processing programs. You can change fonts, text size, alignment, tabs, and indents.

1. Click a text item in the book outline.

2. Format the text using these options:

    - **Change the font color, size, or style.** Select the text you want to change. Click **Format>Character**. The Font window opens. Make the necessary changes and click **OK**.

    - **Change the amount of space between lines of text.** Select a paragraph. Click **Format>Paragraph**. On the Formatting and Indents tab, choose a spacing option from the **Line spacing** drop-down list. Click **OK**.

    - **Change the indent of a paragraph.** Select a paragraph. Click **Format>Paragraph**. On the Formatting and Indents tab, choose new indents from the **Left** and **Right** drop-down lists. Click **OK**.

    - **Add a page break.** Place your cursor where you want the page break to occur. Click **Format>Paragraph**. On the Frame and Page Breaks tab, click the **Page break before** checkbox. Click **OK**.

    - **Change the document's tabs.** Click **Format>Tabs**. The Tabs window opens. Make the necessary changes and click **OK**.

Adding Images

What family history book would be complete without photos, letters, historical records, and maps? Family Tree Maker lets you add images from your family tree or images you've stored on your computer that you don't necessarily want to keep in your family tree—for example, clip art or embellishments.

1. Click a text item in the book outline.

2. Place your cursor where you want the image to appear.

3. Do one of these options:

   • To use an image in your tree, choose **Insert>Image from Media Collection**. The Find Media Item window opens. Select the image and click **OK**.

   • To use an image on your computer, choose **Insert>Image from File**. Navigate to the image you want and click **Open**.

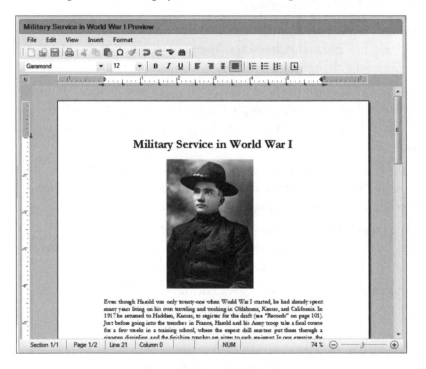

Note: You can also add images linked to individuals by clicking the Media button on the Smart Story toolbar (for more information see page 59). Select the image you want and drag it to your document.

4. To align the image right-click it. Then choose "Left," "Center," or "Right" from the **Justify Image** drop-down list. You can also move the image by dragging it to a new location.

5. To resize an image click it. Then drag one of its square handles to change the size. To maintain the image's proportions, drag the image from one of its corners.

Adding a Chart or Report

You can add as many charts and reports to a book as you'd like. Make sure you choose ones that are appropriate for your audience. For example, you may want to share more personal and informal reports in a book meant for your children, but you'll want to remove facts about living relatives if you are sharing the book with other genealogists.

1. Access the book you want to add a chart or report to.

2. In the book panel toolbar, click the **Add Book Item** (+) button.

3. In the Add Book Item window, click the category for the chart or report you want to use. Then double-click the chart/report, or select its icon and click **OK**.

    Tip: You can also click **Saved Charts** or **Saved Reports** to use items you've already created.

4. Use the editing panel to customize the chart or report (for instructions see chapters 9 and 10).

Adding a Placeholder

If you want to incorporate a story, chart, or photo from outside Family Tree Maker, you can use a placeholder to reserve a specific number of pages until you're ready to add the information.

1. Access the book you want to add a placeholder to.

2. In the book panel toolbar, click the **Add Book Item** (+) button.

3. In the Add Book Item window, click **Other**. Then double-click **Place Holder**, or select its icon and then click **OK**.

4. Choose the number of pages you want to reserve from the **Number of pages** field.

    Tip: Give the placeholder a descriptive name so you don't forget what you were going to use it for. You can change its name by clicking the Book Item Properties button in the book panel toolbar.

Creating a Table of Contents

Family Tree Maker can generate a table of contents for a book automatically. If you make changes to a book (such as adding a chart or moving a chapter), the table of contents and its page numbers will be updated to reflect the changes.

Note: The table of contents is added after the title page. You can change the order of the front matter—table of contents, dedication, preface, etc.—but you cannot move the table of contents out of the front matter.

1. Access the book you want to add a table of contents to.

2. In the book panel toolbar, click the **Add Book Item** (+) button.

3. In the Add Book Item window, click **Other**. Then double-click **Table of Contents**, or select its icon and then click **OK**. The table of contents opens.

    Although you cannot edit the table of contents, you can customize its font, size, and color by clicking the Fonts button under the "Table of Contents Options" heading.

Creating an Index of Individuals

Family Tree Maker can automatically generate a list of all individuals in the book's reports and charts (names mentioned in text items will *not* be included). If you make changes to the book (such as adding a new chart) Family Tree Maker will update the index to reflect the change.

Note: The index cannot be moved; it must be the last item in your book.

1. Access the book you want to add an index to.

2. In the book panel toolbar, click the **Add Book Item** (+) button.

3. In the Add Book Item window, click **Other**. Then double-click **Index**, or select its icon then click **OK**. The index opens.

Although you cannot edit the index, you can customize its font, size, and color by clicking the Fonts button under the "Index Options" heading.

Organizing a Book

As your book grows, you may find that it has changed from the project you originally envisioned and that you need to make some adjustments. Perhaps you've uncovered additional records and photos and you want to rearrange a couple of chapters to include them. Family Tree Maker makes it easy to change titles, move chapters, or even delete sections you don't need.

Changing an Item's Settings

A Family Tree Maker book is made up of a variety of different book items: text items, charts, reports, etc. You can change settings for each book item.

1. Click an item in the book outline.

2. In the book panel toolbar, click the **Book Item Properties** button.

3. Change the item's settings using these options:

   • **Change the item's title.** Enter a title in the **Item name** field. This is the title that will appear in the book's table of contents and this item's headers and footers.

   • **Make this item start a new chapter.** Click the **This item begins a chapter** checkbox.

   • **Make the first page of this item start on an odd-numbered (right-facing) page.** Click the **Start this item on an odd numbered page** checkbox. Typically each chapter starts on an odd-numbered page.

   • **Prevent a page number from appearing on the first page of an item.** Click the **Do not print page number on the first page** checkbox. Typically chapter openers do not include a page number. You may also want to use this option for reports, charts, and full-page images.

   • **Display headers in the item.** Click the **Include the header in this item** checkbox.

- **Display footers in the item.** Click the **Include the footer in this item** checkbox.

4. Click **OK**.

Rearranging Book Items

The book panel shows all the items in a book. The order in which they're displayed in this outline is the order in which they'll print. You can change this order at any time.

1. Click the item you want to move in the book outline.

2. To change an item's order in the outline, select the item. Then click the **Move Up** and **Move Down** buttons in the book panel toolbar. (You can also drag items to the desired location.)

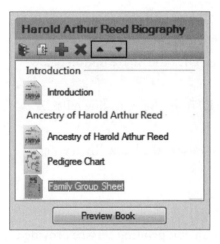

Deleting a Book Item

If you don't want a text item, report, or chart in your book, you can delete it.

1. Click the item you want to delete in the book outline.

2. Click the **Delete Book Item** button.

Printing a Book at Home

When you're done creating a book, you can make copies on your home printer.

Tip: If you want to see what your book will look like before it is printed, click the **Preview Book** button below the book outline.

1. Access the book you want to print.

2. Click the **Print** button below the main toolbar.

3. When prompted choose a printer, select the number of copies, and choose a page range.

4. Click **Print**.

Exporting a Book

You can export your book as a PDF or text file and take it to a copy shop to be printed and professionally bound or email it to family members.

1. Access the book you want to export; then click the **Share** button below the main toolbar.

2. Choose **Export to PDF** or **Export to RTF** from the drop-down list. A file management window opens.

3. Navigate to the location where you want to save the book. Then enter a name for it and click **Save**.

MyCanvas

MyCanvas is a Web-based publishing program and printing service provided by Ancestry.com. After you upload your tree to Ancestry.com, MyCanvas gets you started by automatically generating pages (pedigree trees, family group sheets, and timelines) based on information in your tree. You can then modify these pages by adding photos, stories, historical records, and more. You can also add your own pages or delete pieces you don't like. When you're finished the book can be professionally printed and bound—an heirloom to be enjoyed and shared for years to come.

How Does MyCanvas Work?

MyCanvas is one of the many offerings from Ancestry.com, the parent company of Family Tree Maker. If you've already created a family tree using Ancestry.com or Family Tree Maker, you can use this tree for your project and let MyCanvas do the work for you. The information in your tree will be placed in professionally designed templates. You can leave the pages "as is" or use the interactive tools to add additional photographs, embellishments, and text.

When you complete your book, you may want to print some pages on your desktop printer. Keep in mind, if you choose to print at home, pages will have a low resolution (meaning text and images won't look sharp), and if you have lots of colorful photographs and backgrounds, you can go through quite a bit of ink or toner. Through MyCanvas, you can buy a high-resolution copy of your book and have it printed, professionally bound, and sent to your door.

Note: This guide only explains how to upload your tree to MyCanvas; to learn how to use the tool, go to www.ancestry.com and click the **Publish** button on the main toolbar. Under "Support" click **Help** to view tips and tricks and instructional videos.

Creating a MyCanvas Book

To create a MyCanvas book, you'll need to upload your tree to MyCanvas and create a project. You can create as many books as you'd like—maybe even one book for each branch of your family.

Note: To upload a tree you must be a registered user or have a subscription to Ancestry.com. You must also be connected to the Internet.

1. Go to the **Collection** tab on the Publish workspace.

2. In **Publication Types**, click **Books**. Then double-click **Create a Professionally Printed Book Online**. The Upload to Ancestry window opens.

3. Change any upload options as necessary. If you need help see "Uploading a Tree to Ancestry.com" on page 202.

4. When your tree is uploaded, continue with the next task, "Setting Up a MyCanvas Book."

Setting Up a MyCanvas Book

1. On Ancestry.com click the **Publish** button in the main toolbar. Then click **Family History Books** on the left navigation panel.

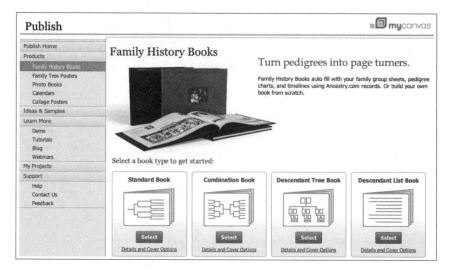

2. Click the icon for the type of book you want to create (standard, combination, or descendant). You can click the "Details and Cover Options" link to learn more about each book type.

   You can now choose a few options for your book.

3. Choose the book's size and the number of generations included.

4. Choose the family tree you want to use. (Because you just uploaded your tree from Family Tree Maker, this should be the default tree selected.)

5. Start typing the name of the individual you want to be the primary person in your tree. The tool will try to recognize the name as you enter it. To use the suggested name, click it in the drop-down list.

6. Enter a name for your book project in the **Name your project** field.

7. Click **Continue**. If prompted, choose a theme for your book. The book project opens.

    You can now use the MyCanvas publishing tool to create your book. Your book project is saved automatically every five minutes; however, make sure you save your project before closing the tool.

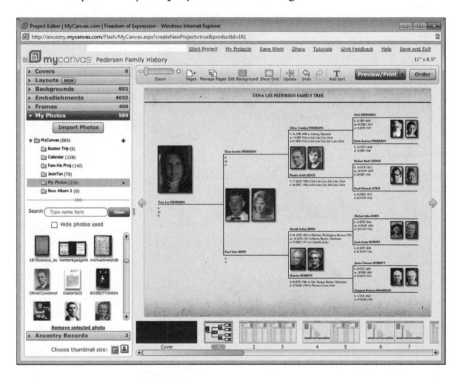

Viewing a MyCanvas Book

Note: You must be connected to the Internet to view a MyCanvas book.

1. Go to the **Collection** tab on the Publish workspace.

2. In **Publication Types**, click **Books**. Then double-click **Go to Existing Online Projects**. A Web browser opens, and the My Projects page is displayed.

3. In the center of the window, you'll see thumbnail images of your projects. Use the arrow buttons to scroll through them. When you find the project you want, click its thumbnail. The MyCanvas publishing tool opens in a new window.

Part Four
Managing Your Trees

Chapter Twelve
Working with Trees

In chapter 3 you learned how to create and import new trees. This chapter explains the many tools Family Tree Maker has to help you manage, share, and protect your trees.

Managing Your Trees

This section explains how to manage your trees effectively, whether you're working on one comprehensive tree or multiple trees.

Opening a Tree

When you launch Family Tree Maker, it automatically opens the last tree you were working in. You can switch to a different tree when necessary.

1. On the main toolbar, click the tree drop-down list and choose the tree you want to open.

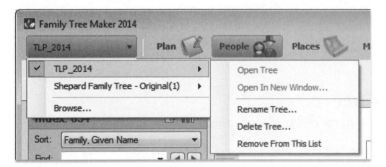

If the tree you want isn't in the drop-down list, click **Browse** to look for it on your hard drive. Navigate to the tree you want and click **Open**.

Note: If you try to open a GEDCOM, a file from a previous version of Family Tree Maker, or a file from another genealogy program, the software automatically opens the New Tree tab so you can import it (for instructions see "Importing a Tree" on page 25).

Viewing Information About a Tree

You can view a summary of your tree, such as its size and the last day you created a backup. You can also see information about the people in your tree, for example, the number of marriages, individuals, and surnames.

1. Go to the **Current Tree** tab on the Plan workspace. A basic summary of your file appears at the top of the tab.

2. To see additional statistics, click the **More** button. The File Statistics window opens.

Renaming a Tree

You can change the name of a tree at any time.

1. On the main toolbar, click the tree drop-down list. Mouse over the tree and click **Rename Tree**.

2. Enter a new name for the tree and click **OK**.

Deleting a Tree

1. On the main toolbar, click the tree drop-down list. Mouse over the tree and click **Delete Tree**.

2. If you want to delete the media files that are linked to the tree, click **Move selected linked files** and select the files you'd like to delete. Then click **OK**.

3. If the tree you're deleting is linked to an online tree, you'll be prompted to delete that tree also. Click **Yes** to delete the online tree; click **No** to keep the tree.

Using Privacy Mode

If your tree contains personal information about living family members, you might want to "privatize" your tree before exporting a family history book or printing a family tree chart. In privacy mode information about living individuals, such birth dates, will not be displayed. Be aware that you cannot edit the tree until you turn off privacy mode.

1. Click **File>Privatize File**. "Privatized" appears in the window's title bar and a checkmark appears next to the Privatize File option in the File menu.

2. To continue working in your tree, turn off privacy mode by clicking **File>Privatize File** again.

Exporting a Tree File

If you want to share your family tree with someone, you can export all or part of a tree as a GEDCOM—the standard file format used to transfer data between different genealogy software. (Be aware that images, audio files, and videos cannot be included in GEDCOMs.) You can also export your tree as a Family Tree Maker file; however, it will be compatible only with the version it was created in.

Tip: To export a specific branch of your family tree, go to the People workspace. Select the person whose family you want to export. Right-click and choose **Export Branch**.

1. Click **File**>**Export**. The Export window opens.

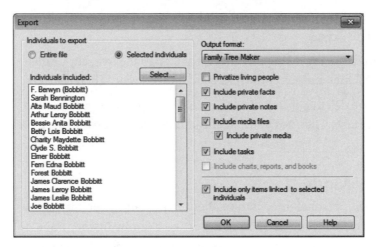

2. Do one of these options:

   - If you want to export the entire tree, click **Entire file**.
   - If you want to choose specific individuals to include in the file, click **Selected individuals**. The Filter Individuals window will open. Click a name and then click **Include** to add the person. When you're finished choosing individuals, click **OK**.

3. Choose a GEDCOM or Family Tree Maker option from the **Output format** drop-down list.

4. Choose the information you want included in the export file:

   - **Privatize living people.** Click this checkbox to exclude information about living individuals. Names and relationships will be exported, but facts and shared facts will not.
   - **Include private facts.** Click this checkbox to export facts marked as private.
   - **Include private notes.** Click this checkbox to export notes marked as private.
   - **Include media files.** Click this checkbox to export all media files in your tree. Click the **Include private media** checkbox to export media items marked as private.

     Note: This option is not available for GEDCOMs.

> **GEDCOM**
>
> Because your great-aunt may not use the same software you do, you'll need to share your family history with her in the GEDCOM format. GEDCOM stands for GEnealogical Data COMmunications; it allows genealogy files to be opened in any genealogy software program—on Macs or PCs.

- **Include tasks.** Click this checkbox to export your research to-do list.

  Note: This option is not available for GEDCOMs.

- **Include charts, reports, and books.** Click this checkbox to export charts, reports, and books you've saved.

  Note: This option is not available for GEDCOMs.

- **Include only items linked to selected individuals.** Click this checkbox to export *only* tasks, notes, and media items that are linked to the individuals you're exporting.

5. Click **OK**. An export window opens.

6. Navigate to the location where you want to save the file.

   Note: Family Tree Maker automatically gives the exported file the same name as the original tree. If you want to use a different name, you can change it.

7. Click **Save**. A message tells you when your file has been exported successfully.

Backing Up Tree Files

Your family trees are important; not only do they contain your family's history, they represent hours of hard work. Unfortunately, computer files can be corrupted by viruses or accidentally deleted. You can preserve your family history through regular backups. Then, if your original tree is damaged or you want to revert to a previous copy, you can restore it from the backup.

Tip: Family Tree Maker can back up a tree automatically every time you exit the program. To do this, click **Tools>Options** and make sure the **Automatically back up family file** checkbox is selected.

Backing Up a File

1. Make sure the tree you want to back up is open and click **File>Backup**. The Backup window opens.

2. If you want a new name to distinguish your backup file from your original tree, enter a new name in the **Backup file name** field. For example, if you back up your trees to the same rewriteable CD every time, and this backup file has the same name as the file that is already on the CD, then this backup will write over the original file.

3. Choose one of these backup types:

    *   **CD, DVD, or flash drive.** Click **Removable Media**. In the drop-down list, choose your CD-ROM drive, DVD drive, or flash drive.

        Note: The first time you back up a file to a CD-ROM, you may get a message asking you to install a driver.

    *   **Hard drive.** Click **Working directory** to save the backup to the folder where your current tree is saved; click **Custom directory** to choose a new location on your hard drive.

4. Choose the information you want to include in the backup:

   - **Media files.** Click this checkbox to include all media items.
   - **Historical events.** Click this checkbox to include historical events you've created or edited for timelines.
   - **Web favorites.** Click this checkbox to include your favorites list on the Web Search workspace.

5. If the tree is linked to an online tree, click **Allow restored file to resume syncing** so the backup file can be synced with the online tree if necessary.

6. Click **OK**. A message tells you when the file has been backed up successfully.

   Note: Backup files cannot be opened in other genealogy programs like GEDCOMs can. They can only be opened in the version of Family Tree Maker in which they were created.

Restoring a File from a Backup

If you need to use your backup file as your working tree, you can restore it when necessary.

1. Disable any anti-virus software running on your computer.

2. If your backup file has been copied to a CD or other removable media, copy it back to your hard drive.

3. Click **File>Restore**. A file management window opens.

4. Navigate to the backup file you want to restore and click **Open**.

   Note: You can identify a backup file by its file extension (the letters after the file name). Family Tree Maker backups use .ftmb.

The tree will open. Any info you entered in the original tree since you created this backup will not be included. Don't forget to reenable your anti-virus software.

Compressing a Tree File

As you work in a tree you will add and delete quite a bit of information. However, even when you delete info, the file size may not change. You should compress a tree periodically to remove unnecessary bits of data and optimize performance.

1. Click **Tools**>**Compact File**. The Compact File window opens.

2. To back up your file before you compress it, click the **Back up file before compacting** checkbox (recommended).

3. Click **Compact**. If you chose to back up your file, the Backup window opens. Change any options as necessary and click **OK**.

4. When Family Tree Maker is finished, a message shows how much the file size was reduced. Click **OK**.

   Because file compression happens behind the scenes, you won't see changes in your tree, but you should notice better performance and a smaller overall file size.

Uploading a Tree to Ancestry.com

Chapter 3 explains how to start a new tree by downloading an existing tree on Ancestry.com. Family Tree Maker also lets you upload a tree to Ancestry.com. It's easy, free, and because your tree will be online, it can be shared with family around the world.

Note: To upload a tree to Ancestry.com, you do not need a subscription, but you must register your copy of Family Tree Maker and have Internet access.

Uploading and Linking a Tree to Ancestry.com

When you upload a tree to Ancestry.com, you can create a link between your desktop Family Tree Maker tree and its corresponding tree on Ancestry. This means that additions, deletions, or edits you make in your Family Tree Maker tree will be duplicated in your Ancestry tree (and vice versa). (For more information see "Working with Linked Trees.")

Be aware that the time it takes to upload your tree is determined by tree size and the speed of your Internet connection. Your tree will be transmitted in two stages. Facts are uploaded immediately. Media items are processed in the background; it may take awhile for them to appear in your online tree.

Note: When you upload and link a tree to Ancestry, you must upload your entire tree; you can't choose which part of your tree is uploaded.

1. Open the tree you want to upload to Ancestry.com. Then go to the Plan workspace and click the **Current Tree** tab.

2. Click the **Upload and Link to Ancestry** button.

3. Enter a name in the **Ancestry tree name** field. To make your tree public, click the **Allow others to see your tree** checkbox.

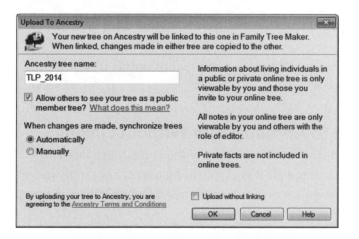

Note: If your tree is private, Ancestry subscribers can still see names, birth dates, and birthplaces from your tree in search results. However, to see

Privacy Options for Ancestry Member Trees

When you upload your tree to Ancestry.com, you can choose between two levels of privacy:

- **Public.** If your tree is public, Ancestry subscribers can view your entire tree (except information about living individuals and private notes), and your tree will appear in search engines such as Google.
- **Private.** If your tree is private, limited information about individuals in your tree (name, birth year, birthplace) will appear in Ancestry search results, but no one can view your entire tree unless you invite them to. Additionally, you can exclude your tree from appearing in search results on Ancestry or third-party search engines such as Google.

your full tree or any attached photos and records, they'll have to ask you for permission. If you don't want your tree to appear in search results either, click the **Exclude from Ancestry search index** checkbox.

4. Choose whether your online and desktop trees are synced manually or automatically. (For more information on synchronization options, see "Setting Up Syncing.")

5. Click **OK**. A message lets you know when the tree has been uploaded successfully.

6. To view your tree on Ancestry.com, click the **View online tree now** checkbox and click **OK**.

Uploading a Tree to Ancestry.com Without Linking

You may want to upload your tree to Ancestry without creating a link between it and your desktop tree. For example if you're creating a poster or family history book in MyCanvas and you plan on deleting the tree when you finish the project.

Note: When you upload a tree without linking it to Family Tree Maker, you can choose which individuals are included in the tree.

1. Open the tree you want to upload to Ancestry.com.

2. Click the **Share** button on the main toolbar and choose **Upload to Ancestry**.

3. Click the **Upload without linking** checkbox and click **OK**. The Upload to Ancestry window opens.

4. Do one of these options:

   - To upload the entire tree, click **Entire file**.

   - To choose specific individuals to include in the tree, click **Selected individuals**. The Filter Individuals window will open. Click a name; then click **Include** to add the person. When you're finished choosing individuals, click **OK**.

5. Choose what information you want in your Ancestry tree:

   - **Privatize living people.** Click this checkbox to exclude information about living individuals. Names will be replaced with the word "Living." Relationships will be uploaded, but facts and shared facts will not.

   - **Include private facts.** Click this checkbox to upload facts marked as private.

   - **Include private notes.** Click this checkbox to upload notes marked as private.

   - **Include media files.** Click this checkbox to upload all media files in your tree. Click the **Include private media** checkbox to upload media items marked as private.

6. Click **OK**. A browser window opens.

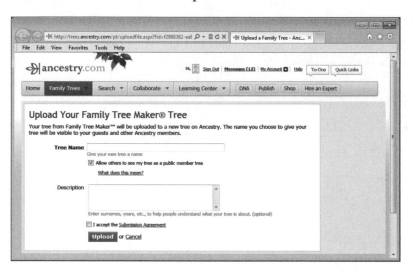

7. Enter a name in the **Tree Name** field. To make your tree public and view-able by all Ancestry subscribers, click the **Allow others to see my tree** checkbox.

Note: If your tree is private, Ancestry subscribers can still see names, birth dates, and birthplaces from your tree in search results. However, to see your full tree or any attached photos and records, they'll have to ask you for permission.

8. Click the checkbox to accept the submission agreement and click **Upload**. Ancestry.com opens and displays your tree.

Differences Between Desktop and Online Trees

Most content in your tree is uploaded and/or synced seamlessly between Family Tree Maker and Ancestry. However, because the trees are in different formats, there are a few differences you should be aware of.

Content	Differences
Facts	In general fact dates, places, and descriptions (including alternate facts) are the same in Family Tree Maker and Ancestry trees. However, some fact types have different labels. For example, the Physical Description fact in Family Tree Maker is the Description fact in Ancestry trees.

Content	Differences
Media items	• The caption of a media item in Family Tree Maker is the same as the Picture name field on Ancestry. • Audio and video items are not transferred between Family Tree Maker and Ancestry. • Media items attached to relationships in Family Tree Maker are not uploaded to Ancestry. • Ancestry records you've merged into Family Tree Maker won't be re-uploaded to Ancestry. • Documents can't be uploaded to Ancestry trees in these formats: .exe, .dll, .bat, .htm/.html, and .mht. • Photos that exceed 15MB will be resized when uploaded to Ancestry—your original file will not be affected. Images need to be in one of these formats: .jpeg, .bmp, .png, .gif, or .tif.
Notes	In Family Tree Maker you can create a variety of notes: person, research, fact, relationship, media, and source citation. All notes are uploaded, but only person notes can be viewed or edited online.
Places	Shortened display names and GPS coordinates in Family Tree Maker are not included in Ancestry trees.
Publications	Saved reports, charts, and books cannot be transferred from Family Tree Maker to Ancestry.
Relationships	In Family Tree Maker only you can view information you've entered for a living individual. In your Ancestry tree, anyone you give permission to can view information about living individuals.
Sources	• Sources created with templates will transfer to Ancestry, but you cannot edit them online. • Media items attached to citations are uploaded; media items attached to sources are not.
Stories	• A story created on Ancestry.com will become an .htm file in Family Tree Maker, which can be viewed in a Web browser. You can edit the text in a word-processing program. • Smart Stories created in Family Tree Maker will be text files (.rtf) in Ancestry. The story can't be viewed in your Ancestry tree but the document can be downloaded. (Smart Stories are uploaded only if they are attached to individuals.)

Working with Linked Trees

Family Tree Maker makes entering information into your tree fast and easy. It also contains robust tools to help you organize your media items, cite sources, and create charts and reports. But because the program is on your desktop, sharing your tree with others can be time-consuming, and, if you don't have a laptop, you won't have access to your tree on the go.

Fortunately TreeSync™ gives you the freedom to view and update your tree no matter where you are. First, create your tree in Family Tree Maker. Then upload and link it to Ancestry.com. When you go to the library or a family member's home—anywhere with Internet access—make changes to your tree online. Then sync the changes to your desktop tree when you get home. (You can also download and link a tree you've already created on Ancestry.com. For information see "Downloading a Tree from Ancestry.com" on page 26.)

TreeSync also makes it easy to share your tree with friends and family. Simply send an email invitation and relatives around the world can view your tree (and even collaborate with you) without any software or an Ancestry subscription.

Setting Up Syncing

When you link your desktop and online trees together, you can choose how your trees will be synchronized. You have two options:

- **Automatically.** Family Tree Maker checks for changes when you open a tree or close the program. If it detects differences between the trees, it synchronizes the changes automatically. You can also sync your trees any time by clicking the Sync Now button on the Current Tree tab.

- **Manually.** You can synchronize your trees by clicking the Sync Now button on the Current Tree tab or choosing "Sync Now" from the sync icon in the main toolbar.

You can also choose whether or not Family Tree Maker will display a list of changes you've made to your online and desktop trees that you can review before syncing.

Changing Your Current Sync Setting

When you upload or download a linked tree, you will choose how your trees will be synced. You can change this setting at any time.

1. Go to the **Current Tree** tab on the Plan workspace.

2. Click the **Sync Now** button and choose "Sync Options" from the drop-down. The Update Options window opens.

3. Click **Automatically** or **Manually**.

4. To download images of historical records from Ancestry when your trees sync, click the **Download citation media from Ancestry** checkbox.

5. Click **OK**.

Creating a Log of Recent Sync Changes

You can set up TreeSync so that every time you sync your online and desktop trees you can view a list of recent changes—the number of people, sources, and media items that have been added, updated, or deleted from your tree since the last sync.

1. Go to the **Current Tree** tab on the Plan workspace.

2. Click the **Sync Now** button and choose "Sync Options" from the drop-down. The Update Options window opens.

3. Click the **Show Change Log before finalizing sync** checkbox. Then click **OK**. The next time your trees are synced, you'll see the Sync Change Log.

Sync Change Log	Added	Changed	Deleted
Changes from Ancestry: TLP_2014			
People	0	4	0
Media	1	0	0
Sources	4	0	0
Citations	4	0	0
Changes from Family Tree Maker: TLP_2014			
People	0	3	0
Citations	1	0	0

View / Print Details   Sync will continue in 57 seconds. (Stop Timer)

☐ Don't show 'Change Log' during sync   Continue   Cancel Sync   Help

4. To proceed with the sync, click the **Continue** button. To reject the changes, click the **Cancel Sync** button. You can also click the "Stop Timer" link if you want time to review the changes; click the **View/Print Details** button to see specific details about what changes will be included in the sync.

Viewing a Tree's Sync Status

The sync icon in the upper-right corner lets you see at a glance whether your desktop and online tree are synced. A check mark icon means that the trees are up-to-date; an icon with two vertical arrows means that you have changes waiting to be synced (fig. 12-1).

Figure 12-1. Left, trees are in sync; right, trees need to be synced.

You can also see the date and time when your tree was last synced on the Current Tree tab on the Plan workspace.

Syncing Trees Manually

You can sync your tree manually at any time. However, be aware that you can't work in your online or desktop tree until synchronization is complete. This may take a few seconds to a few minutes.

On the Plan workspace, click the **Current Tree** tab; then click the **Sync Now** button. On other workspaces, click the sync icon and choose "Sync Now" from the drop-down.

Note: You can't sync your trees from Ancestry.com; you must use Family Tree Maker. To see the changes in your online tree, you'll need to reload or refresh the Ancestry.com website in your Web browser.

Resolving Conflicts Between Linked Trees

When you change the same fact in your desktop and online trees, you'll need to choose which information to keep (fig. 12-2). For example, if you change a birthplace in Family Tree Maker and a family member changes the same birthplace in your Ancestry tree, when you try to sync your trees, you'll be prompted to fix the issue.

Resolve Conflicts

There are conflicting changes between the data in Family Tree Maker and the data in your linked online tree at Ancestry.

Item (2)	Description	Change
Person	Sarah Ann Gold (1854 - 1925)	Birth
Person	Francis Gold (1858 -)	Baptism

- ⦿ Resolve conflicts manually
- ○ Overwrite conflicts with Family Tree Maker data
- ○ Overwrite conflicts with Ancestry data

[Continue...] [Cancel Sync] [Help]

Figure 12-2. A message showing conflicts between linked trees.

1. Do one of these options:

   • To keep the information entered in Family Tree Maker, click **Overwrite conflicts with Family Tree Maker data**.

   • To keep the information entered in the Ancestry tree, click **Overwrite conflicts with Ancestry data**.

   • To manually choose which information to keep, click **Resolve conflicts manually**.

2. Click **Continue**. If you are overwriting data, the sync continues. If you are resolving the conflict manually, choose the facts you want to keep and click **Continue** again.

   Important: Deletions always take priority over other changes. For example, if you delete an individual in your online tree and update the same individual's birthplace in your desktop tree, when you sync the trees together the individual will be deleted.

Unlinking Trees

If you no longer want your desktop and online trees linked together, you can remove the connection between them.

Warning: If you unlink your desktop and online trees, changes will no longer be synchronized, and you cannot relink the trees.

1. Go to the **Current Tree** tab on the Plan workspace.

2. Click the **Sync Now** button and choose "Sync Options" from the drop-down. The Update Options window opens.

3. Click **Unlink trees** and click **OK**.

4. When prompted, enter your Ancestry account password and click **Unlink**.

   Tip: You can also unlink your trees on the website. Go to Ancestry.com and click the **Family Trees** tab at the top of the window. Then click the "Manage tree" link next to the appropriate tree. On the Tree Settings page, click the **Unlink Tree** button.

Changing Privacy Settings

When you upload a tree to Ancestry.com, you choose whether your online tree will be public (the default) or private. However, you can change its privacy settings at any time. (For more information on the differences between public and private trees, see page 204.)

1. Go to the **Current Tree** tab on the Plan workspace.

2. Click the **Sync Now** button and choose "Manage Online Tree Privacy" from the drop-down. The Tree Settings page opens.

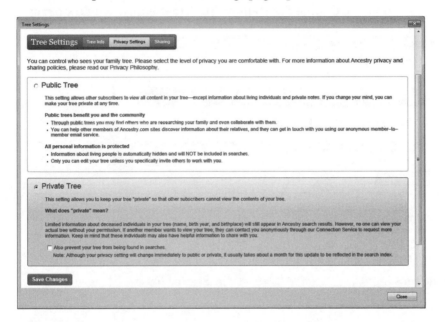

3. Click **Public Tree** to let other Ancestry.com subscribers view your tree; click **Private Tree** to prevent others from viewing your tree.

    Note: If your tree is private, Ancestry subscribers can still see names, birth dates, and birthplaces from your tree in search results. However, to see your full tree or any attached photos and records, they'll have to ask you for permission. If you don't want your tree to appear in search results either, click the **Exclude from Ancestry search index** checkbox.

4. Click **Save Changes**.

Inviting Others to View Your Tree

You can invite friends and family to view your Ancestry.com tree. You can even let them add new information or photos.

Warning: Anyone assigned the role of "editor" can add, edit, or delete information in your online tree. These changes will be made to your desktop tree when the trees are synced together.

1. Go to the **Current Tree** tab on the Plan workspace.

2. Click the **Invite to Online Tree** button. The Tree Settings window opens.

Note: If you've already invited people to your tree, you'll need to click the **Sync Now** button and choose "Manage Online Tree Invitees" to invite more people to your tree.

3. Click the **Invite people** button. Complete the invitation and assign the person one of these roles: editor, contributor, guest.

4. If you want, include a personal message to the invitee. Then click **Send Invites**.

Roles in Ancestry Member Trees

When you invite people to view your tree, they can participate in different ways, depending on the role you assign them:

- **Editor.** Editors can add, edit, or delete anyone in your tree, add stories and photos, and leave comments. They can also see living individuals. Editors cannot delete or rename the tree, change tree settings, or invite others to the tree.
- **Contributor.** Contributors can add photos or stories to your tree, but they cannot add or edit people. You can choose whether or not they see living individuals.
- **Guest.** Guests can only view your tree and leave comments. You can choose whether or not they see living individuals.

Chapter Thirteen
Tools and Preferences

Using Family Tree Maker Tools

If you need some extra help calculating birth dates, understanding how individuals are related to each other, or creating a to-do list, Family Tree Maker has several tools that can help.

Soundex Calculator

Soundex is a term familiar to serious family historians. It's a coding system used by the government to create indexes of U.S. census records (and passenger lists) based on how a surname sounds rather than how it is spelled. This was done to compensate for potential spelling and transcription errors. For example, "Smith" may be spelled "Smythe," "Smithe," or "Smyth." Using Soundex, these "Smiths" are all identified by the same code (S530). You can use Soundex to find surnames that use the same code and then search for ancestors using all these surname variations.

Click **Tools**>**Soundex Calculator**. Then enter a surname in the **Name** field, or click **Index** to select someone in your tree.

Relationship Calculator

The relationship calculator helps you identify how two people in your tree are related, shows an individual's nearest common relative, and gives his or her canon and civil numbers.

Note: Canon and civil numbers indicate the degree of relationship between individuals. Canon laws (used in the United States) measure the number of steps back to a common ancestor. Civil degree measures the total number of steps from one family member to another.

1. Click **Tools>Relationship Calculator**. In the first field you'll see the home person. In the second field you'll see the individual who is the current focus of the tree.

2. To change the individuals whose relationship you're calculating, click the **Person from people index** button next to a name (the button with an index card). In the Index of Individuals window, select a new person and click **OK**.

The individuals' relationship is listed underneath their names. If they have multiple connections (for example, if they are cousins who married), click the drop-down list to see each relationship. You can also see how the individuals are related in the Path section.

Date Calculator

You can use the date calculator to figure out an individual's birth year, age at the time of a specific event, or the date of an event. For example, if you know the date your grandmother was married and you know how old she was when she got married, you can determine the approximate year she was born.

1. Click **Tools>Date Calculator**. The date calculator opens.

2. Use this chart to help you enter dates into the calculator:

To calculate this	Do this
A birth date	• Click **Birth date**. • Enter a date in the **Date of known event** field. • Enter the individual's age in the **Age at time of event** fields.
The date of a specific event	• Click **Other event date**. • Enter a date in the **Known birth date** field. • Enter the individual's age in the **Age at time of event** fields.
An individual's age on a specific date	• Click **Age**. • Enter a date in the **Known birth date** field. • Enter a date in the **Date of known event** field.

3. Click **Calculate**. The calculated event date or age appears.

Name Converter

If you import another person's genealogy file into your tree, you may find that each file has recorded names differently; your surnames may be in all caps while their's may not. You can use the convert names tool to format all names in your tree at once.

1. Click **Tools**>**Convert Names**. The Convert Names window opens.

2. To capitalize the first letter in each name, click **First Middle Surname**. To capitalize the first letter of the first and middle names and capitalize the entire surname, click **First Middle SURNAME**.

3. Click **OK**.

Find Individual Tool

You can use any fact in your tree (such as occupation or burial) to locate either a specific individual or a group of individuals who fit specific criteria. For example, you can search for everyone in your tree who lived in Illinois at the time of the 1850 census. Or, you can find out which individuals are buried in the same cemetery.

Note: The Find Individual tool searches Place and Description fields; Date fields cannot be searched.

1. Click **Edit**>**Find Individual**. The Find Individual window opens.

Find Individual			
Birth ▼	Kentucky		Find

Name	Birth Date	Death Date	
John W. Bobbitt	09 Jun 1832	23 Aug 1909	
Cyntha Ann Haggard	21 Dec 1807	25 Feb 1885	
Dawson Haggard	01 Jun 1793	1828	
Louesa Haggard	1813	1838	
Louisa Haggard	1813	1884	
Melvina Haggard	1808	13 Mar 1880	
James A. Shanklin	06 Sep 1810	29 Oct 1887	
Sarah Bennington	17 Feb 1812	13 Aug 1863	
William Bennington Shanklin	1838	Bef. 1870	
Margaret Jane Shanklin	1850	Aft. 1880	
Joseph A. Shanklin	1842	Bef. 1880	
Ann E. Shanklin	1840	Bef. 1880	

Count: 30 · Go To · Close · Help

2. Choose the type of fact you want to search from the drop-down list. Then enter your search term and click **Find**.

3. If you want to view a specific individual, click his or her name in the search results and click **Go To**.

Automatic Reference Numbers

Some family historians use reference numbers to identify people in their trees, particularly if the tree contains individuals with identical names. Family Tree Maker can assign reference numbers to individuals (Person ID), relationships (Relationship ID), or both.

Note: If you have entered your own reference numbers, Family Tree Maker will not overwrite them.

1. Click **Tools>Options**. Then click the **References** tab.

2. Click **Use individual reference numbers** to choose how numbers are assigned to individuals; click **Use relationship reference numbers** to choose how numbers are assigned to relationships.

3. Click **Numbers only** to assign numbers, starting with 1. Click **Prefix** to add a prefix before the number (you can enter numbers, letters, and/or symbols). Click **Numbers plus suffix** to add a suffix after the number (you can enter numbers, letters, and/or symbols).

4. Click **OK**.

Global Birth Order Tool

In the family group view, you can change the order in which children are displayed in a family by clicking the Move up and Move down buttons. If you always want to display children in your tree by birth order, you can use this tool to change them all at once.

1. Click **Tools>Sort All Children by Birth**.

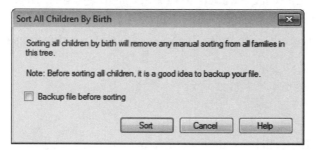

2. If you want to back up your file before you sort children, click the **Back up file before sorting** checkbox (recommended).

3. Click **Sort**.

Research To-Do List

Whether you are a new user or an experienced family historian, the to-do list can help you keep track of the research you've already done and create tasks for your next steps. You can add research tasks for specific individuals or general tasks for your entire tree; tasks can be as simple as sending an email to a cousin or as complicated as locating an entire family in the 1940 census.

Creating a To-Do Task

When you create a task, you can choose the priority of the task, the category it fits in, and its due date.

Note: This section explains how to add tasks for specific individuals. You can also add tasks to the tree's to-do list on the Current Tree tab on the Plan workspace.

1. Go to the **Person** tab for a specific individual (on the People workspace). Click the **Tasks** tab.

2. Click the **New** button in the tasks toolbar. The Add Task window opens.

3. Enter the task in the **Description** field. For example, "Look for Madeline's birth information in Highland, Utah."

4. Click **Edit** to choose a category for the task. Choose a category or create a category and click **OK**. (For more information see the next task, "Creating Task Categories.")

5. Choose a deadline for the task from the **Due date** drop-down list. Then choose a priority. (Assign a high priority to the tasks you want to accomplish first.) When you're finished click **OK**.

   Tip: You can print the to-do list for this individual by clicking the Print button on the tasks toolbar. To print a list of all tasks in your tree, use the Task List report on the Publish workspace.

Creating Task Categories

Each task you create can be assigned to a category. Family Tree Maker has a set of default categories, but you can add ones that are useful to your research.

1. Go to the **Current Tree** tab on the Plan workspace. In the Tasks section you can see your current to-do list.

	Tasks: 6				Go To
	Task Description	Task For	Category / Location	Due	Created
	High Priority				
☐ ❗	Get military family tree printed for reunion		Reeds	6/17/2013	6/24/2013
	Medium Priority				
☐ ⊖	Check for new DNA matches			7/1/2013	2/2/2013
☐ ⊖	Look for burial information in Dawson, ...	John W. Bobbitt	Bobbitts	8/5/2013	5/24/2013
	Low Priority				
☐ ⬇	Find Brighton church yearbook at FHL		Family History Library	8/1/2013	6/24/2013
☐ ⬇	Scan Grandpa Pete's journal		Pedersens	9/30/2013	7/24/2013

2. Click **New**. The Add Task window opens. Click **Edit**. The Category/Location window opens, showing all available categories.

Category / Location

Task:

Categories:
- ☑ Bobbitts
- ☐ Communication
- ☐ Family History Library
- ☐ Gedges
- ☐ Pedersens
- ☐ Reeds
- ☐ Scanning

OK · Cancel · Help · Add... · Edit... · Delete · Clear · Reset

3. Click **Add**. The Add Category Name window opens.

4. Enter a name in the **Category name** field and click **OK**. Click **OK** again.

Marking a Task as Complete

When you finish a task on your to-do list, you'll want to mark it as complete. Go to the **Current Tree** tab on the Plan workspace. In the Tasks section, click the checkbox next to the task.

Tip: To delete a task, click its name; then click the red (X) button in the tasks toolbar.

Sorting the To-Do List

You can filter the to-do list in various ways. For example, you can sort the list to show which tasks are done or still pending.

1. Go to the **Current Tree** tab on the Plan workspace.

2. Click the **Filter tasks** button and choose one of these options from the drop-down list:

    • To show every task you've entered, choose **Show All Tasks**.

    • To show unfinished tasks choose **Show Uncompleted Tasks**.

    • To show tasks that belong to a specific category, choose **Filter by Task Categories**.

Tip: You can change what information is displayed for each task. Click the **Show/Hide columns** button in the tasks toolbar. Then, from the drop-down list, select or deselect specific columns.

Setting Up Preferences

Family Tree Maker is a powerful program with many features and options. To get the most out of the software, you might want to take a minute and define a few key preferences.

General Preferences

You can set some preferences that affect the interface and general workings of Family Tree Maker.

1. Click **Tools**>**Options**. Then click the **General** tab.

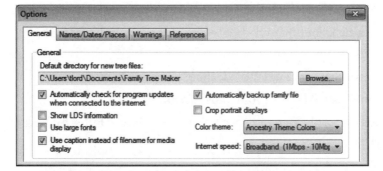

2. Change the general preferences as necessary:

    *   **Default directory for new tree files.** To change the default location where trees are saved on your hard drive, click **Browse** and choose a new folder.

    *   **Automatically check for program updates when connected to the Internet.** Click this checkbox if you want Family Tree Maker to look for software updates when you're online. You'll be alerted if an update exists.

    *   **Show LDS information.** Click this checkbox if you want to display LDS facts such as sealings and baptisms.

    *   **Use large fonts.** Click this checkbox to make fonts in the software larger and more readable.

        Note: A larger font may help readability, but some labels may not display correctly or may be cropped.

- **Use caption instead of file name for media display.** Click this check-box to sort media items by the captions you've given them; otherwise media items will be sorted and displayed by file name.

- **Automatically back up family file.** Click this checkbox to create backups of your trees automatically when you close the program. If your original tree is ever lost or damaged, you can use the backup to restore your information.

- **Crop portrait displays.** Click this checkbox to resize portrait images so that they fill the frame on the editing panel.

  Note: The actual images in your tree will not be modified. Also, you cannot choose to resize individual thumbnails. This option resizes every portrait in your tree.

- **Color theme.** Choose the color theme you want from the drop-down list: default for Ancestry is light green; Windows is classic blue; or you can select your current Windows display.

- **Internet speed.** Choose the Internet connection you're using from the drop-down list.

- **PDF driver.** If you don't want to use the default PDF driver, you can choose your own from the list.

Fastfields Preferences

Fastfields speed up data entry by automatically filling in repetitive data as you type. For example, if you type "San Jose, California, USA" into a place field then go to another place field and begin to type "San," Family Tree Maker will recognize the similarity and suggest "San Jose, California, USA." By default, all Fastfields are used, but you can turn off any you'd like.

1. Click **Tools>Options**. Then click the **General** tab.

2. In the Use fastfields for section, click the checkboxes for each type of field you want to turn off Fastfields for: names, places, sources, and/or fact descriptions.

Fastfields

Fastfields save you time by automatically filling in some types of information. Perhaps you noticed as you typed an individual's name that the last name was completed for you. This is because name fields, among others, are Fastfields.

Location Fastfields remember the places you've entered in a tree. As you type a location, Family Tree Maker suggests possible matches. Use the keyboard arrows or mouse to highlight the correct location and press Enter to select it. You can also keep typing a name to override the Fastfields suggestion.

Online Searching Preferences

You can determine whether or not Family Tree Maker will search Ancestry.com for matching records and trees when you're connected to the Internet.

1. Click **Tools**>**Options**. Then click the **General** tab.

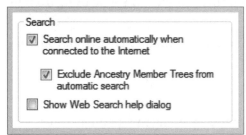

2. Change these preferences as necessary:

   • **Search online automatically.** Click this checkbox to have Family Tree Maker search Ancestry.com for individuals in your tree when an Internet connection is available.

   You'll see a green leaf (or hint) next to an individual when possible matches have been found. If you deselect this feature, you can still search Ancestry for your family members on the Web Search workspace.

   • **Exclude Ancestry Member Trees from automatic search.** Click this checkbox if you don't want hints from Ancestry.com Member Trees.

- **Show Web Search help dialog.** Click this checkbox to display Web Merge help when you begin an online search.

Spell Checking Preferences

You can choose which terms the spell check should ignore. By default these include words in uppercase and HTML tags.

Tip: You can use the dictionary to add unusual family surnames or locations that you want the spell checker to ignore.

1. Click **Tools**>**Options**. Then click the **General** tab.

2. Click the **Spell Check Options** button.

Fact Display Preferences

The editing panel on the Person tab includes a Sources tab. If you want, you can also display media and notes tabs.

1. Click **Tools**>**Options**. Then click the **General** tab.

2. In the Fact display section, click the checkbox for each type of tab you want to display on the person editing panel.

Date Preferences

Family Tree Maker lets you change how dates are formatted.

1. Click **Tools**>**Options**. Then click the **Names/Dates/Places** tab.

2. Change these date preferences as necessary:

- **Date display format.** Choose how dates are displayed. Click **Day Month Year** to show the day before the month (07 January 2014). By default, Family Tree Maker displays dates in this accepted genealogical date standard. Click **Month Day Year** to show the month before the day (January 7, 2014).

Click the drop-down lists to choose different formats for the day, month, and date separator.

- **Double dates.** Change the year in this field to change the default double date cutoff year. If you do not want double dates to print, set the double date cutoff year to zero.

Note: Calendars in Europe and the United States changed in 1752—moving from Julian to Gregorian. In the Julian system the first day of the year was 25 March. In today's Gregorian system 1 January is the first day of the year. Dates that fall between January and March of 1752 can be interpreted in two ways, and some genealogists prefer to show both dates. For example, February 22 could fall in the year 1750 according to the Gregorian calendar, so the date would be noted as 22 February 1750/51.

- **Fact labels.** To display a different abbreviation for the term "About" (meaning "circa"), enter your preferred label.

- **Ancient date notation.** Choose whether dates before 100 AD are displayed with BC/AD or BCE/CE.

Name Preferences

Family Tree Maker lets you determine how names are displayed in the Index on the People workspace. You can include titles, alternate names, and married names for females.

1. Click **Tools>Options**. Then click the **Names/Dates/Places** tab.

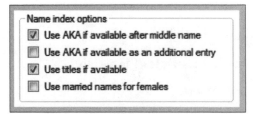

2. Change these preferences as necessary:

- **Use AKA if available after middle name.** Click this checkbox to have Also Known As names included with the preferred name (for example, Bobbitt, Mary Eliza "Mollie").

- **Use AKA if available as an additional entry.** Click this checkbox to give Also Known As names their own entries in the Index (for example, Hannah Willis and Anna Willis).

- **Use titles if available.** Click this checkbox to have titles included with the preferred name (for example, Hoyt, Captain Samuel).

- **Use married names for females.** Click this checkbox to list women by their married (and maiden) names (for example, Hoyt, Maria Hitchcock).

Place Preferences

Family Tree Maker lets you determine whether place names entered in your tree are compared against the software's location database.

1. Click **Tools>Options**. Then click the **Names/Dates/Places** tab.

2. Change these preferences as necessary:

- **Check place authority when entering place names.** Click this check-box to have Family Tree Maker compare each place you enter against its database of locations. This keeps your locations in standard formats and consistent throughout your tree.

- **Exclude selected country from resolved place names.** When you enter a place name, you usually include a country. However, if most events occur in the same country (for example, if most of your ances-tors were born and died in England), you may not want to include that country's name in place fields and charts and reports. To keep a country's name from appearing, choose it from the drop-down list.

Warning and Alert Preferences

Family Tree Maker can automatically check your tree for problems and alert you if it detects a possible error, such as unusual dates.

1. Click **Tools**>**Options**. Then click the **Warnings** tab.

2. Change these warning preferences as necessary:

   - **Show alerts for unlikely birth, death, and marriage dates.** Click this checkbox to get alerts when you enter dates that don't seem accurate (for example, a death date that occurs earlier than a birth date).

   - **Show unrecognized place name indicators.** Click this checkbox to get alerts when Family Tree Maker doesn't recognize a location you've entered.

     Note: This option is not available if you deselected the "Check place authority" option on the General tab.

   - **Show informational alerts.** Click this checkbox to get alerts when you update your tree—for example, when you change the home person or edit an individual's name.

- **Show prompt when sorting children in the family view.** Click this checkbox to get alerts when you manually sort children in the family group view.

- **Show backup reminder before critical operations.** Click this checkbox to be reminded to back up your tree before completing tasks like merging duplicate individuals.

The Show warnings for non-critical errors section lets you choose how you want Family Tree Maker to handle minor errors:

- **Double dates.** If Family Tree Maker detects double dates, you can leave the dates as they are, use formatting to show both dates, or be prompted for instructions.

- **Titles in name fact.** If Family Tree Maker detects titles such as Jr. or Sr. in a Name fact, you can leave the title in the Name fact, move the title to the Title fact, or be prompted for instructions.

- **One- or two-digit years.** If Family Tree Maker detects years entered with one or two digits, you can accept the date as it is, change the date to the most recent century, or be prompted for instructions.

- **Text in quotes.** If Family Tree Maker detects nicknames (indicated by quotes) in a Name fact, you can leave the nickname in the Name fact, move the nickname to the AKA fact, or be prompted for instructions.

- **Copy media files.** When you add a media file to your tree, you can choose whether or not to automatically copy the file to the Family Tree Maker media folder or be prompted for instructions.

- **Auto-populate Smart Stories.** When you create a Smart Story, you can start with a blank page, a page populated with information about the individual and his or her family, or be prompted for instructions.

Managing Facts

Facts are the essential building blocks of your tree, where you record the details about your family. In order to capture the information you care about, you might want to create your own facts or change which fields appear in predefined facts.

Creating a Custom Fact

You can create custom facts that work for your family tree. For example, if you are tracking your ancestors by census records, you can make a custom fact for each census year.

1. Click **Edit>Manage Facts**. The Manage Facts window opens.

2. Click **New**. The Add Custom Fact window opens.

3. Change the fact as necessary:

   - **Fact label.** Enter the name of the fact as it will appear on the Person tab.

   - **Short label.** Enter a short name (up to six characters) for the fact that will appear on the Tree tab editing panel.

   - **Abbreviation.** Enter an abbreviation (up to three characters) for the fact that will appear in reports.

   - **Fact type.** Choose **Individual fact** if the fact applies to one person, such as birth or death. Choose **Shared fact** if the fact applies to more than one individual, such as marriage.

- **Fact options.** Choose the fields that you want to appear for the fact: Date and Place; Date, Place, and Description; or Description only.

- **Private by default.** Click this checkbox to make this fact type private. You can change privacy for a specific fact on the Person tab.

- **Fact sentence.** To change the default sentence, see "Modifying a Fact Sentence."

4. Click **OK**.

Modifying a Predefined Fact

While you can't rename or delete predefined facts, you can choose which fields are included as part of the fact. For example, you can modify the Cause of Death fact so that only the Description field is included.

1. Click **Edit>Manage Facts**. The Manage Facts window opens.

2. Click the predefined fact that you want to modify. Then click **Properties**. The Fact Properties window opens.

3. In **Fact options** choose the fields you want for the fact.

4. Click the **Private by default** checkbox to make this fact type private. You can change privacy for a specific fact on the Person tab.

5. Click **OK**.

Modifying a Fact Sentence

When you create an Ahnentafel, descendant report, or Smart Story, Family Tree Maker generates descriptive sentences for each fact or event. You can change the wording and choose what info is included. For example, the default burial sentence looks like this: Robert Gedge was buried on 1 Sept 1888 in Attleborough, England. If you record cemetery names, you could add this to the sentence: Robert Gedge was buried in the All Saint's Cemetery in Attleborough, England, on 1 Sept 1888.

1. Click **Edit>Manage Facts**. The Manage Facts window opens.

2. Click **New** or select the fact you want to modify and click **Properties**. The Fact Properties window opens. The Fact sentence field displays the current sentence—a combination of text and predefined data variables.

3. To change the text, simply add, delete, or type over it. To change which variables are in the sentence, delete the variable or choose a new one from the **Insert Fact Data** drop-down.

    Tip: If you don't like your changes and want to use the default sentence, click **Insert Fact Data** and choose **Reset Fact Sentence**.

    The Example field shows what the fact sentence will look like. For example, if you deselect the Description checkbox, you can see what the sentence will be if the Description field for the fact is blank.

Managing Historical Events

An individual's timeline and the Timeline report can include historical events. You can edit or delete any historical event. You can also add entries that are relevant to your family history, such as international events that caused your ancestors to immigrate.

1. Click **Edit>Manage Historical Events**. The Manage Historical Events window opens.

2. To delete an event, click the entry; then click **Delete**.

3. To add an event click the **New** button. The Add/Edit Historical Event window opens.

4. Change the historical event as necessary:

   - **Event title.** Enter a short title for the event.

   - **Event date.** Enter the date of the event.

   - **Place where event occurred.** Enter a location for the event.

   - **Category.** Choose a historical category from the drop-down list or add your own categories. You can also edit and delete the default categories.

   - **Description.** Enter a summary of the historical event.

5. Click **OK**.

Customizing the Tree Tab Editing Panel

By default, these facts appear on the editing panel of the Tree tab in the People workspace: name, sex, birth date and place, death date and place, marriage date and place. If you often record burials or christenings, you can add these facts to the editing panel so you can enter the information more easily.

1. Go to the **Tree** tab on the People workspace. The editing panel appears with its default facts.

2. Click **Customize View**. The Customize View window opens.

3. In the Individual facts section or the Shared facts section, click the fact you'd like to add to the editing panel; then click the right arrow button to add the fact to the Selected facts sections.

4. To change the order in which facts display on the panel, click a fact in the Selected facts section and click the up and down arrows.

5. Click **OK**. The editing panel now includes the new facts.

Entering User Information

You can enter information that identifies you as the creator of a tree. This info is automatically added to your file if you export and send it to another family member or researcher.

1. Click **Tools**>**User Information**. The User Information window opens.

2. Enter your information and click **OK**.

Chapter Fourteen
Family Tree Problem Solver

No matter how organized you are or how carefully you enter information, errors can creep into your tree. Whether you've added a child to the wrong family or spelled your ancestor's name incorrectly, Family Tree Maker makes it easy to clean up your tree.

Straightening Out Relationships

At some point in your research you may discover that a certain individual doesn't belong in your tree and you need to delete him or her. Or maybe you added a child to the wrong family. Cleaning up relationship issues as soon as you find them keeps them from multiplying.

Merging Duplicate Individuals

After months and years of gathering names and dates, your family tree may become a bit disorderly. You might discover that Flossie and Florence are actually the same person. If you've entered duplicate individuals, you should merge them together (instead of deleting one) so that you don't lose any information.

Family Tree Maker can assess your tree and show you individuals who might be duplicates.

Note: Before you merge individuals, make a backup of your tree. If you need help see "Backing Up a File" on page 200.

Finding Duplicate Individuals

After adding a lot of new information or merging a family member's tree with yours, it's a good idea to check for duplicate individuals.

1. Click **Edit>Find Duplicate People**. The Find Duplicate People window opens.

Person 1	Person 2	Match Score
Hoyt, Captain Benjamin (1802 -)	Hoyt, Benjamin (1801 -)	1000
Gedge, Mary (1862 - 1862)	Gedge, Leah (1860 - 1862)	990
Perry, Martha (1836 -)	Perry, Margaret (1838 -)	990
Spangler, Maurine (1895 - 1986)	Spangler, Leila M. (1890 -)	990
Lucas, Mary Peak (1806 - 1860)	Lucas, Charity Peak (- 1849)	990
Bobbitt, Winny (1778 -)	Bobbitt, Amy (1785 -)	990
Main, Unknown (1797 -)	Main, Deborah (1799 -)	857
Lucas, John Peak ()	Lucas, Elijah Peak ()	848
Bobbitt, William ()	Bobbitt, William (1761 -)	606
Bennington, Rebecca ()	Bennington, Mary Elizabeth (1794 - 1864)	517
Lucas, Thomas Peak ()	Lucas, Singleton Peak (1810 - 1877)	429

Total Matches: 11   Go To Person   Remove Row   Compare/Merge...   Close   Help

In the Person 1 and Person 2 columns you'll see the individuals who might be duplicates. (You can click a column header to sort a column alphabetically.) In the third column you'll see a match score—the higher the number the more likely the individuals are a match; a 1,000 means the individuals are almost exact matches.

2. To merge a pair of individuals (or just compare the two), click their row in the window and click **Compare/Merge**. The Individual Merge window opens. To complete the merge, continue with step 5 in the next task, "Merging Individuals."

Merging Individuals

If you discover that two individuals in your tree are actually the same person, you can merge the two together and retain all the facts and sources associated with each person.

1. Go to the **Tree** tab on the People workspace and click the name of one of the duplicate individuals in the Index.

2. Click **Person>Merge Two Specific Individuals**. The Index of Individuals window opens.

3. Click the name of the other duplicate individual. You can use the scroll bar to move up and down the list, or you can type a name (last name first) in the **Find** field.

4. Click **OK**. The Individual Merge window opens.

    The two columns show the facts attached to each individual. You can decide how the information is merged together and whether you want to keep or discard alternate facts.

5. Use the buttons next to the facts to determine how each fact will be merged:

    *   To keep a fact and mark it as preferred, select the button next to the fact. The corresponding fact for the other individual will be merged as an alternate fact unless you discard it.

    *   To remove a fact, click the Alternate arrow and choose "Discard" from the drop-down list. Though you may discard any fact you like, it is usually a good idea to keep all facts in case they turn out to be relevant.

        If you discard a fact, you can include its sources and media items by clicking the **Keep sources** checkbox.

        Note: To learn more about preferred and alternate facts, see "Adding Alternate Facts" on page 42.

6. Click **OK** to complete the merge.

Removing an Individual from a Tree

If you've mistakenly added an individual who isn't related to you, don't worry, Family Tree Maker makes it easy to delete the individual and his or her information from your tree.

1. Go to the **Tree** tab on the People workspace.

2. Make sure the individual you want to delete is the focus of the Index and family group view.

3. Click **Person>Delete Person**. A message asks you to confirm that you want to delete the individual. Click **Yes**.

All notes, tasks, and media links associated with the person will be permanently deleted.

Note: Whenever you want to remove someone permanently from your tree, always use the Delete Person menu option. If you try to delete someone by removing his or her name from the Name fact, you won't actually delete the individual—or any of his or her facts or relationships.

Removing a Marriage

As you continue your research you might find that you've connected a couple incorrectly. You'll need to delete any marriage facts you've entered and also detach the individuals from each other.

1. Go to the **Tree** tab on the People workspace and select the appropriate couple.

2. Click the **Person** tab for one of the individuals. Right-click the **Marriage** fact and choose **Delete Fact**. A message asks if you want to delete this fact (and associated notes) from both individuals. Click **Yes**.

    Note: If you don't delete the Marriage fact, the individual will still be considered married but to an unknown person.

3. To detach the individual from the current spouse, click **Person>Attach/ Detach Person>Detach Selected Person**. The Detach window opens.

4. Click the checkbox for the incorrect spouse. If the couple has children, you can click their checkboxes to detach them from the selected individual too.

5. Click **OK**.

Detaching a Child from the Wrong Parents

If you've added a child to the wrong parents, you can detach the child from the family without deleting them from your tree.

1. Go to the **Tree** tab on the People workspace.

2. Make sure the correct family is the focus of the family group view. Then click the child's name.

3. Click **Person>Attach/Detach Person>Detach Selected Person**. The Detach window opens.

4. Click the checkboxes next to the father and/or mother.

5. Click **OK**.

Attaching a Child to a Father and Mother

If you've added an individual and his or her parents to your tree, but you did not know they were related when you entered them, you can still link them together.

1. Go to the **Tree** tab on the People workspace.

2. Make sure the individual you want to attach to his or her parents is the focus of the Index or family group view.

3. Click **Person>Attach/Detach Person>Attach Mother/Father**. The Select the Mother/Father to Attach window opens.

4. Choose the father or mother from the list and click **OK**. If the father or mother has multiple spouses, you'll need to choose which family the child belongs to.

5. Choose the appropriate family and click **OK**.

Fixing Text Mistakes

It's easy to introduce errors into your tree. Perhaps you transcribed a record too quickly or imported incorrect notes from a family member's tree. Family Tree Maker has several tools that can help look for misspellings, inaccurate dates, and duplicate facts.

Global Spell Checker

The global spell checker lets you search for errors in your tree.

1. Click **Tools>Global Spell Check**.

2. Change these options as necessary:

   • **Fact descriptions.** Click this checkbox to search fact descriptions.

   • **Media.** Click this checkbox to search media captions and descriptions.

   • **Sources.** Click this checkbox to search citation detail and citation text fields.

   • **Notes.** Click to search all notes.

   • **Tasks.** Click to search all task in the research to-do list.

3. Click **Begin Checking**. If the spell checker finds a potential error, it displays the word in the "Not in dictionary" field.

4. Replace or ignore the word using the spell check buttons. A message tells you when the spell check is complete, click **OK**.

Find and Replace Tool

You may have mistakenly spelled an individual's name wrong throughout your tree or perhaps you abbreviated a place name that you want to spell out now. You can use Find and Replace to correct these mistakes—one by one or all at the same time.

1. Click **Edit>Find and Replace**. The Find and Replace window opens.

2. Enter the term you want to search for in the **Find** field. Then enter the new term you want to use in the **Replace with** field.

3. Choose one or more of these options:

   • To find words that match your search exactly (uppercase and lowercase), select the **Match case** checkbox.

- To find entire words that match your search, select the **Find whole words only** checkbox. (For example, a search for Will would not show results for William or Willton.)

- To search using wildcards, click the **Use wildcards** checkbox. Wildcards allow you to search for one or more missing characters. An asterisk (*) replaces multiple characters; a search for "Mas*" could find Massachusetts, Masonville, or Masterson. A question mark (?) replaces one character; a search for Su?an would find Susan and Suzan.

4. Click the checkbox for each part of the tree you want to search in. If you're not sure where the information is, you might want to select all of the checkboxes.

5. Click **Find**. The first result that matches your terms appears.

6. If you want to replace the current match, click **Replace**.

   Tip: You can replace all matching search results by clicking the **Replace All** button. Before you do, back up your file because you cannot undo these changes.

7. To find the next matching term, click **Find Next**.

8. Continue searching and replacing terms as necessary.

Merging Duplicate Facts

If you have multiple versions of the same fact, you can merge them together. You can choose only one date and place for the fact. If you have multiple descriptions, they will be combined into one.

1. Go to the **Person** tab on the People workspace and select the appropriate individual.

2. Click the **Facts** button.

3. Right-click one of the duplicate facts and select **Merge Duplicate Facts**. The Merge Duplicate Facts window opens.

4. Click the checkboxes next to the facts you want to merge and click **Next**.

5. Select the date and location you want to keep.

6. Click **Finish**.

Running the Data Errors Report

Family Tree Maker can search your tree and identify potential errors. For example, it can look for blank fields or date problems, such as an individual being born before his or her parents were born. It's a good idea to run the Data Errors Report periodically to make sure your tree is as error free as possible.

1. Go to the **Collection** tab on the Publish workspace. In Publication Types, click **Person Reports**.

2. Double-click the **Data Errors Report** or click the report icon and then click the **Detail** tab.

3. To determine which errors the report lists, click the **Errors to include** button on the editing toolbar. The Errors to Include window opens.

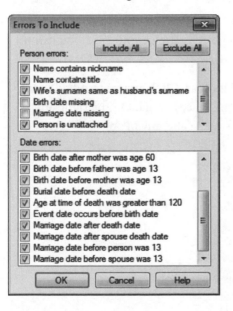

4. Click the checkboxes next to the errors you want to search for. Then click **OK**. The Data Errors Report opens.

5. To fix the error immediately, simply click an individual's name in the report. An editing window will open.

Standardizing Locations

When you import a tree or manually enter a location, Family Tree Maker checks the location against its database of three million places. If any misspellings are found, or if the place doesn't match any sites in the database, a location is considered "unidentified."

You'll want to examine these "unidentified" locations occasionally and make any necessary changes. In some cases, you'll want to leave the name exactly as it is. For example, if a town or city no longer exists, or the county boundaries have changed over the years, you'll want to keep the location's name as it is. However, in most cases, you'll want to identify locations to keep your tree consistent and to make sure that locations are grouped together correctly on the Places workspace.

Identifying a Single Location

If you see a question mark icon next to a place name in your tree, you can try to identify the place in the locations database.

1. Click the **Places** button on the main toolbar. Click an unidentified location (with a question mark icon) in the Places panel. On the right side of the window, you'll see the location's name and any people and events associated with it.

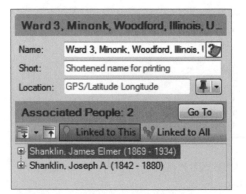

2. Click the question mark icon next to the location's name.

3. Choose one of these options:

    • If a suggestion matches the location in your tree, click its name in "Suggested place names" and click **Replace**.

- If no locations are a match, you can ignore only part of a location by clicking the **Move to place detail** arrow. When the updated location finally has a match, click **Replace**. (You can also click **Ignore** to leave the location as it is.)

    Note: Ignoring part of a location doesn't change how it is displayed in your tree; it simply allows the location to be grouped together correctly on the Places workspace.

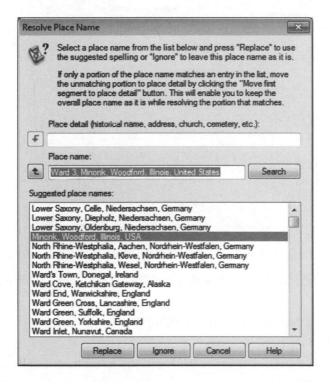

Identifying Multiple Locations

If you've imported a tree or merged someone's tree into your own, you'll likely have many place names that don't match the other locations in your tree. Instead of updating each location one at a time, you can identify multiple locations at once.

1. Click **Tools>Resolve All Place Names**.

2. To back up your file before you update your locations, click **Yes**. The Backup window opens. Change any options as necessary and click **OK**.

    The Resolve All Place Names window opens. Each unidentified location is listed, along with a suggested replacement location.

3. For each listed location, click the checkbox for the option you want to use:

    • **Unrecognized Place Name.** Click this checkbox to leave the location as it is.

    • **Suggested Place Name.** Click this checkbox to change the current location to the suggested location.

    • **Desc.** Click this checkbox to move the location's name from the Place field to the Description field.

    • **Ignore.** Click this checkbox to leave the location as it is. The location name will no longer be "unidentified."

    • **Other.** To see other locations that might match the current place name, or to ignore only part of a location, click **Other**. The Resolve Place Name window opens. When you identify a matching location, click **Replace**.

4. When you've chosen an option for each location, click **OK**.

Finding Missing Media Items

If you move a media item on your computer after you've added it to a tree, you won't be able to view, print, or export the item until it is relinked to your tree. You can search for missing media items individually or all at once.

Finding a Single Missing Media Item

On the Media workspace the editing panel shows the media item's name and location on your computer. If a media item is no longer linked to your tree, you'll see a red "File not found" message (fig. 14-1). To relink the media item, click the link and locate the item.

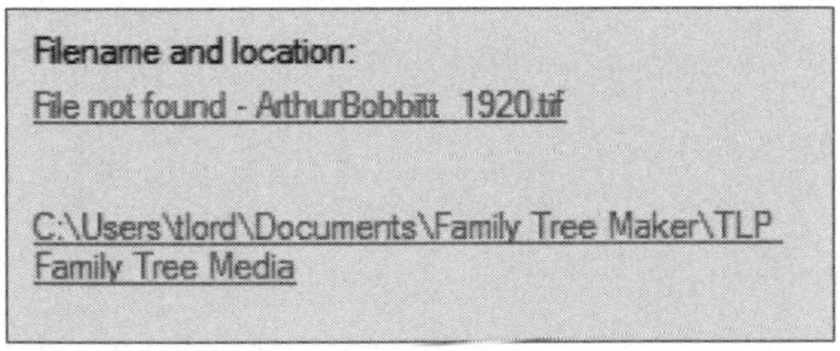

Figure 14-1. A missing media file.

Finding All Missing Media Items

1. Click the **Media** button on the main toolbar. Click **Media>Find Missing Media**. A list of unlinked images appears.

2. Click the checkboxes next to the items you want to locate or click **Select All** to find all broken media links.

3. Click **Search**. If Family Tree Maker finds the file, its current location is displayed in the Path column; a check mark appears in the Status column. If Family Tree Maker can't find the file, it will be highlighted. Click an item to search for it yourself.

4. When you're finished, click **OK**.

Troubleshooting

Although we hope you never have problems while using Family Tree Maker, all computers and software have their own incompatibilities. This chapter identifies several common problems and includes ways to fix them.

If you don't find an answer to your question, you can get help at www.familytreemaker.com/support. Click the "Visit the Knowledge Base" link. Enter your issue in the **Keyword Search** field and click **Search**.

When dealing with technical issues, you should make sure that your computer meets or exceeds the system requirements. Also, keep in mind that the more information you enter, the greater the amount of free hard drive space and available RAM you will need. If you plan to include many pictures, audio, or video files in your trees, you will need a substantial amount of hard drive space.

LEGAL DISCLAIMER

IMPORTANT—READ CAREFULLY BEFORE FOLLOWING TROUBLESHOOTING TIPS

Family Tree Maker has made every effort to make the information contained in this guide accurate, complete, and useful. However, inaccuracies, errors, and omissions may occur. All recommendations, statements, and procedures are given without warranty of any kind. The user assumes all risks associated with use of this guide.

Ancestry.com Issues

Because Family Tree Maker and Ancestry.com are closely linked together, you may encounter some website-related issues when using Family Tree Maker.

When I try to access a record on Ancestry.com, I see an error message. What does it mean?

Occasionally you may come across one of these error messages:

Document contains no data.

503 Service Unavailable.

We're sorry, this page is temporarily unavailable.

These types of errors usually indicate a temporary issue with your Internet Service Provider (ISP) or the Ancestry.com website. To resolve the issue refresh or reload the Web page by pressing **CTRL+F5**. Or you can try to view the page again later.

If you keep seeing the same error message, you should clear your temporary Internet files. For instructions go to the Family Tree Maker Knowledge Base; then enter "483" in the search field and click **Search**.

I have problems printing and saving information I find on Ancestry.com when I access the website through Family Tree Maker.

The Web Search feature lets you add records from Ancestry and also navigate the entire website. However, some features on Ancestry work better when accessed through a regular Web browser rather than through the Family Tree Maker browser because of its limited functionality. If you're having trouble using an Ancestry feature in Web Search, click the **Browser Options** button (left of the Address field) and choose "Open in New Window" to open the site in a regular Web browser.

Occasionally an Ancestry Hint is blank or I get a message saying that I have no unreviewed hints. How do I get rid of these empty hints?

These "phantom" hints usually mean that you've made a change to your tree, but the changes haven't been communicated to Ancestry yet. You will continue to see these hints until the information is reindexed and added to the website.

Damaged or Corrupt Files

I don't have a backup of my tree and my file won't open. Is there anything I can do?

Files can be damaged by viruses, a merging of corrupt data, the improper shut down of Family Tree Maker, and more. If you don't have a backup of your tree, you can try to fix your current file. For help go to the Family Tree Maker Knowledge Base; then enter "5146" in the search field and click **Search**.

Display Problems

In Family Tree Maker buttons and fields overlap each other and are difficult to read. How can I fix this?

Display problems can occur if you have changed the default Windows font size. You'll need to change your Windows font size, or you can drag open a window to enlarge it. For more information on this issue, go to the Family Tree Maker Knowledge Base; then enter "2937" in the search field and click **Search**.

Error Messages

You may occasionally receive an error message while installing or using Family Tree Maker. Here are some messages you might see:

Authentication with server failed.

This message can appear for several reasons, including an incorrect date and time setting, security conflicts, and Internet connection issues. For instructions on resolving this issue go to the Family Tree Maker Knowledge Base; then enter "3734" in the search field and click **Search**.

Cannot find d:setup.

This message appears when you try to install the software and have selected the wrong drive. To fix this problem, simply select the drive where you inserted the installation DVD.

Family Tree Maker has encountered a problem and needs to close/Family Tree Maker has stopped working.

Usually this message is caused by an old or corrupt Family Tree Maker configuration file. For instructions on deleting this file go to the Family Tree Maker Knowledge Base; then enter "5029" in the search field and click **Search**. If you keep seeing this message, please contact technical support.

Incorrect file version.

This message appears when you're importing a file that is not supported by Family Tree Maker (for example, if someone shares a Family Tree Maker file with you but you're using a different version of the software). For help importing a file go to the Family Tree Maker Knowledge Base; then enter "4363" in the search field and click **Search**.

You are not connected to the Internet or are behind a firewall.

This message appears when your Internet connection is inactive or when something is blocking Family Tree Maker from using your Internet connection. To troubleshoot this issue go to the Family Tree Maker Knowledge Base; then enter "2257" in the search field and click **Search**.

You must be logged on as an administrator.

In Windows you may need to run Family Tree Maker as an administrator. To do this right-click the Family Tree Maker icon and select "Run as Administrator." If you need more help go to the Family Tree Maker Knowledge Base; then enter "3779" in the search field and click **Search**.

File Importing Errors

I get an error message when I try to import a tree.

It is important to determine if the importing problem is specific to one file or to multiple files. If you can import some files but not others, the file may be damaged. You may need to revert to a backup. If you cannot import *any* files, create a new test file in Family Tree Maker and export it as a GEDCOM. Now try to import the test file. If it doesn't import, you'll need to uninstall and reinstall the software. For more information, go to the Family Tree Maker Knowledge Base; then enter "4400" or "4848" in the search field and click **Search**.

I am having trouble importing a large tree file. What can I do?

You can import the tree using a low memory option. This process will copy the file directly to your hard drive instead of using your computer's memory. It will take more time than the standard import but may allow you to import a file you normally wouldn't be able to. For instructions on using the low memory import, go to the Family Tree Maker Knowledge Base; then enter "5233" in the search field and click **Search**.

Installation Problems

For the majority of users, Family Tree Maker installs without any problems. However, if you are experiencing difficulties you should test the DVD on another computer to verify that the disc is good. If the installation DVD is damaged, contact technical support for assistance. If the DVD works on another computer, one of these topics may help you resolve the problem.

I can't get Family Tree Maker to install on my computer.

Occasionally Family Tree Maker won't install on your computer because of conflicts with other software, corrupt user profiles, and other reasons. For help troubleshooting this issue, go to the Family Tree Maker Knowledge Base; then enter "5250" in the search field and click **Search**.

My system locks up during installation and I see the message, "This program has performed an illegal operation and will be shut down."

Close shortcut toolbars and any programs that are running, including antivirus software. Then try reinstalling the software.

Nothing happens when I put the DVD in the DVD drive.

There may be fingerprints, scratches, or dust on your DVD. Remove the DVD from the drive and gently wipe it with a clean towel. Do not wipe in a circular motion; wipe from the inside edge to the outside edge.

The Windows Autorun feature may be turned off. You'll need to start the installation program yourself. Make sure the DVD is in the DVD drive.

- **Windows XP.** Click the Windows **Start** button and select **Run**.

- **Windows 7 and Vista.** Click the Windows **Start** button and select **All Programs>Accessories>Run**.

In the **Open** field, type "d:setup". (The "d" in "d:setup" stands for drive D. If you are installing from another drive, type that letter instead. For example, from drive E, type "e:setup".) Then click **OK**.

I get a message saying there isn't enough hard drive space to install the program.
You may be out of space on the drive where Windows is installed, the drive where you're attempting to save the program, or the drive where your temporary folder is located. To ensure that you have sufficient hard drive space, check the following:

- **Hard drive space available on the drive where Windows is installed.** You need to have at least 675MB of space available on the drive where Windows is installed. In addition, Windows needs at least 150MB of free hard drive space to run properly after Family Tree Maker has been installed. You may encounter problems if you have less.

- **Hard drive space available on the drive where Family Tree Maker is saving your trees.** You generally need to have three times the size of your file available because of the way many Windows programs (including Family Tree Maker) save files. For example, if your file is 400,000 bytes, you actually need 1,200,000 bytes (1.2MB) available to save it.

- **Temporary hard drive space.** Windows has a temporary storage folder, usually C:\Windows\Temp. This folder should be cleaned out on a regular basis. To do this close all open programs. In Windows XP click the Windows **Start** button and select **Run**; in Windows 7 or Vista click the Windows **Start** button and select **All Programs>Accessories>Run**. Then, in the **Open** field, type "temp" and click **OK**. Windows opens the Temp folder. Make sure the window's title bar says "Temp" and delete any files.

I get a message saying, "Cannot find d:setup."
The "d" in "d:setup" stands for drive D. If you are installing from a drive other than drive D, access the correct drive.

I get a message saying, "You must be logged on as an administrator."
In Windows access to common tasks and programs may be managed by the
User Account Control (UAC). If you are trying to access Family Tree Maker as a
standard user (meaning without administrative privileges), you won't be able to
open the program. You will need to run Family Tree Maker as an administrator. If
you need instructions, go to the Family Tree Maker Knowledge Base; then enter
"3779" in the search field and click **Search**.

How do I manually uninstall Family Tree Maker?
If you have uninstalled and reinstalled the Family Tree Maker program and it still
opens with the error message, "Program has encountered a problem and must
close" (or something similar), you may need to manually remove Family Tree
Maker. To troubleshoot this issue (and learn how to uninstall the program), go to
the Family Tree Maker Knowledge Base; then enter "4848" in the search field and
click **Search**.

Internet Connection Problems

*I get an error message that says, "You are not connected to the Internet or are
behind a firewall."*
This error occurs when your Internet connection is inactive, or when something
is blocking Family Tree Maker from using your Internet connection.

Make sure Internet access is enabled in Family Tree Maker. To do this go to the
File menu and select **Go Online**. (If the menu option "Go Offline" appears, Internet access is already enabled.)

Check your Internet connection. If you have a dial-up Internet connection, or
you have disabled your broadband connection, establish your Internet connection before you open Family Tree Maker. Make sure you are able to get to other
websites. If you are still unable to use Family Tree Maker online features, you can
troubleshoot this issue. Go to the Family Tree Maker Knowledge Base; then enter
"2257" in the search field and click **Search**.

PDF Problems

I am unable to save a chart as a PDF.

If you have problems saving reports and charts as PDFs, you may need to designate yourself as an administrator on your computer. If you need instructions, go to the Family Tree Maker Knowledge Base; then enter "3779" in the search field and click **Search**.

Also, be aware that PDFs in Family Tree Maker are limited to 200 inches by 200 inches. If your chart is larger than this, the contents will be cropped.

Performance Issues

Family Tree Maker is running slowly. What can I do?

If Family Tree Maker is running more slowly than expected, here are a few steps you can take to increase the software's performance.

- Make sure your computer meets or exceeds the system requirements.

- Run the Compact File tool to reindex your file and remove unnecessary data. (For instructions see "Compressing a Tree File" on page 202.)

- Check your tree for duplicate individuals or sources. Merge them as necessary.

- Work offline. Consider temporarily disabling Internet access in Family Tree Maker. To do this go to the **File** menu and choose **Go Offline**.

- Turn off Ancestry Hints. To do this go to the **Tools** menu and choose **Options**. Deselect **Search online automatically when connected to the internet** and click **OK**.

- Disable Fastfields. Disabling Fastfields in large databases can also speed things up. To do this go to the **Tools** menu and choose **Options**. Deselect all checkboxes in the Use fastfields for section and click **OK**.

Printing Problems

Many printing problems are related to the specific printer you're using. Before you begin, make sure your printer is hooked up correctly, turned on, and connected to the computer. Also, make sure you're familiar with any documentation that came with your printer. If you don't find your issue in the topics below, you may want to contact technical support for the printer's manufacturer.

I am unable to print in Family Tree Maker.

Try to print an image or document from another program. This will verify whether or not the printer is functioning properly. If you can print something using another program, the issue may be a conflict with Family Tree Maker.

The most common cause of printing issues involves conflicts between the program and printer driver, which acts as a translator between the printer and the program. Verify that the driver for your printer is up to date. Most manufacturers offer these drivers as free downloads from their websites.

Your computer may be running low on memory. Family Tree Maker requires that you have at least 1GB of physical memory to run. If you don't have enough memory, Family Tree Maker might take a long time to perform certain tasks like printing, especially if you have a large tree. Try closing other programs to make more memory available. If the performance is still sluggish, you might want to add more memory to your system.

Why is Family Tree Maker printing slowly?

Printing from Windows, especially when printing graphics, can be slow. To improve your printing speed, try printing images at a lower quality. Be aware that the final product won't look as nice.

The Windows spool settings may be slowing down printing. To disable these features, see your Microsoft Windows user's guide. You may also need to refer to the printer's documentation.

My photos are not printing clearly.

Try changing the image to a different format before you import it. Family Tree Maker accepts a variety of common file formats.

The original image may be of poor quality. If you scanned the photograph, you may need to rescan it.

Family Tree Maker crashes when I print charts and reports.
Verify that the driver for your printer is up to date. Most manufacturers offer these drivers as free downloads from their websites.

Program Unexpectedly Shuts Down
Family Tree Maker may shut down unexpectedly, and you may see an error message.

I get a message saying, "Family Tree Maker has stopped working," or "Family Tree Maker has encountered an error and needs to close."
Usually this message is caused by an old or corrupt Family Tree Maker configuration file. For instructions on deleting this file go to the Family Tree Maker Knowledge Base; then enter "5029" in the search field and click **Search**. If you keep seeing this message, please contact technical support.

Family Tree Maker keeps crashing. What can I do?
All applications, no matter how stable, crash from time to time. However, if Family Tree Maker is crashing frequently you may want to follow the steps outlined below to resolve this issue. Create a backup of your tree before beginning these tasks.

- Confirm that your Windows software is up to date. If you don't know how to do this, see these Microsoft help articles:

  For Windows XP go to http://windows.microsoft.com/en-us/windows-xp/help/setup/set-up-automatic-updates.

  For Vista go to http://windows.microsoft.com/en-us/windows-vista/install-windows-updates.

  For Windows 7 go to http://windows.microsoft.com/en-us/windows7/updating-your-computer.

- Periodically, Family Tree Maker releases updates that fix bugs and add new features. Make sure that Family Tree Maker is up to date by going to the **Help** menu and choosing **Check for Update**.

You can find more information on this issue in the Family Tree Maker Knowledge Base. For Windows XP enter "4442" in the search field and click **Search**; for Vista enter "5157"; and for Windows 7 enter "5158".

Registration Issues

I am having trouble registering the software.

Your computer may not be connected to the Internet. Make sure that you are able to access and sign in to Ancestry.com using a normal Web browser (Internet Explorer, etc.). If you are unable to access the website you'll need to fix your Internet connection first.

Make sure Internet access is enabled in Family Tree Maker. To do this go to the **File** menu and select **Go Online**. (If the menu option "Go Offline" appears, Internet access is already enabled.)

Your firewall settings or security software may be preventing Family Tree Maker from starting the registration process. You may need to add FTM.exe as an exception to your security software or firewall. For information about changing firewall settings, contact your security software manufacturer directly.

Make sure that your computer's date and time are correctly set to your time zone. If you need help, check the user manual for your computer.

Software Updates

How can I make sure I have the latest software updates?

Periodically, Family Tree Maker releases updates that fix bugs and add new features. Make sure that Family Tree Maker is up to date by going to the **Help** menu and choosing **Check for Update**.

You may need to run Family Tree Maker as an administrator in order to check for updates. If you need instructions, go to the Family Tree Maker Knowledge Base; then enter "3779" in the search field and click **Search**.

TreeSync Issues

I get an error message when I try to sync my desktop and online trees.

Occasionally you may get an error message when you try to sync your linked trees. This can occur when your Internet connection is interrupted during the synchronization process. Make sure your connection is working correctly and try syncing your tree again. If you keep having problems, go to the Family Tree Maker Knowledge Base; then enter "5433" in the search field and click **Search**.

———————

Check your Internet connection. If you have a dial-up Internet connection, or you have disabled your broadband connection, establish your Internet connection before you open Family Tree Maker. Make sure you are able to get to other websites. If you are still unable to sync your trees, you can troubleshoot this issue. Go to the Family Tree Maker Knowledge Base; then enter "2257" in the search field and click **Search**.

———————

Make sure Internet access is enabled in Family Tree Maker. To do this go to the **File** menu and select **Go Online**. (If the menu option "Go Offline" appears, Internet access is already enabled.)

I synced my trees and I can't see all the media items in my online tree. What happened?

When you synchronize trees, data is transferred immediately. Media items are processed separately in the background. Because of this it may take a while for all your images to appear in your online tree. You can track the progress of your media sync using the Media processing status bar on the main toolbar.

Glossary

Ahnentafel German for ancestor table. In addition to being a chart, it also refers to a genealogical numbering system.

ancestor A person you descend from—parent, grandparent, great-grandparent, etc.

Ancestry Hint The green leaf indicating that a person might have matching records on Ancestry.com.

Ancestry Member Tree A family tree you have created on or uploaded to Ancestry.com.

blended family A family composed of a couple and their children from previous relationships and/or marriages, as well as any children they have together.

combined family view An option in the family group view that lets you view blended families.

CSV Comma Separated Values. A file format that organizes information into fields and can be imported into a spreadsheet.

descendant A person who descends from you—your child, grandchild, great-grandchild, etc.

editing panel A section of a workspace that lets you easily edit and view information for a specific individual or item.

export To transfer data from one computer to another or from one computer program to another.

family group sheet A chart or report that displays information about a single family—father, mother, and children.

family group view Shows a single family—father, mother, and their children—in Family Tree Maker.

family view One of the display options for the tree viewer on the People workspace. Similar to the vertical pedigree chart.

Fastfields A feature that reminds you of locations and people you've entered previously so that when you type a new place or name, you'll see possible matches.

GEDCOM GEnealogical Data COMmunication. A standard designed by the Family History Department of The Church of Jesus Christ of Latter-day Saints for transferring data between different genealogy software programs.

genealogy report A narrative-style report that details a family through one or more generations and includes basic facts about each member.

generation The period of time between the birth of one group of individuals and the next—usually twenty-five to thirty years.

given name The first (and middle name) given to a child at his or her birth. Also known as a Christian name.

hint See Ancestry Hint.

home person The main individual in your tree.

HTML HyperText Markup Language. The standard language for creating and formatting Web pages.

icon A small picture or symbol that represents a program, file, or folder on your computer. Double-clicking an icon causes the program to run, the folder to open, or the file to be displayed.

import To bring a file into a program that was created using another program.

maternal ancestor An ancestor on the mother's side of the family.

MyCanvas The Ancestry.com Web-based publishing tool and printing service that lets you create books, calendars, and posters.

paternal ancestor An ancestor on the father's side of the family.

PDF Portable Document Format. A file format that retains printer formatting so that when it is opened it looks as it would on the printed page.

pedigree chart A chart that shows the direct ancestors of an individual. Also known as an ancestor tree.

pedigree view One of the display options for the tree viewer on the People workspace. Similar to the standard pedigree chart.

preferred A term Family Tree Maker uses in reference to parents, spouses, or duplicate events indicating that you want to see the preferred selection first or have it displayed in charts and reports.

primary person The individual who is currently the focus of the workspace, chart, or report.

RTF Rich Text Format. A basic text file format that can be opened in almost all word-processing programs.

siblings Children of the same parents.

Smart Stories A tool that helps you compose stories using facts, sources, notes, and images from your tree.

Soundex A system that assigns a code to a surname based on how it sounds rather than how it is spelled.

source Where you found specific information, such as a historical records, a book, or an interview.

source citation The individual details about where information is located within a source.

surname The family name or last name of an individual.

TreeSync™ A feature that lets you link trees from Family Tree Maker and Ancestry.com so that changes made to one tree will be reflected in the other.

Web clipping The ability to "clip" text or images from a Web page and add them elsewhere, like to your Family Tree Maker tree.

Web Dashboard A feature on the Plan workspace that lets you view your Ancestry.com account and trees.

Web Merge A feature that lets you take records you've found on Ancestry.com and add them to your Family Tree Maker tree.

workspace A major grouping of Family Tree Maker features. Each workspace can be opened from the main toolbar.

Index